The Ultimate James Bond Trivia Book

The Ultimate James Bond Trivia Book
A Citadel Quiz Book

Michael Lewis

A Citadel Press Book
Published by Carol Publishing Group

Copyright © 1996 by Michael Lewis

All rights reserved. No part of this book may be reproduced in any form, except by a newspaper or magazine reviewer who wishes to quote brief passages in connection with a review.

A Citadel Press Book
Published by Carol Publishing Group
Citadel Press is a registered trademark of Carol Communications, Inc.

Editorial Offices: 600 Madison Avenue, New York, N.Y. 10022
Sales and Distribution Offices: 120 Enterprise Avenue, Secaucus, N.J. 07094
In Canada: Canadian Manda Group, One Atlantic Avenue, Suite 105, Toronto, Ontario M6K 3E7, Canada

Queries regarding rights and permissions should be addressed to: Carol Publishing Group, 600 Madison Avenue, New York, N.Y. 10022

Carol Publishing Group books are available at special discounts for bulk purchases, sales promotions, fund raising, or educational purposes. Special editions can be created to specifications. For details contact: Special Sales Department, Carol Publishing Group, 120 Enterprise Avenue, Secaucus, N.J. 07094

Manufactured in the United States of America
12 11 10 9 8 7 6 5 4 3 2 1

Library of Congress Cataloging-in-Publication Data

Lewis, Michael (Michael D.), 1962–   .
    The ultimate James Bond trivia book / Michael Lewis.
       p. cm.
    "A Citadel Press book."
    ISBN 0-8065-1793-X (pbk.)
    1. James Bond films—Miscellanea.   I. Title
PN1995.9.J3P46   1996
791.43′651—dc20   95–48089
                                                                         CIP

Preface

With the 1995 release of *GoldenEye,* James Bond celebrated his thirty-third year as one of the most popular fictional heroes in the history of motion pictures. Few could have imagined in 1962, when production began on the modestly budgeted *Dr. No,* that 007 would be an international icon going into the next century. Credit for the success of the Bond series belongs to many people—the talented producers, directors, and technicians, the writers, and the five actors who have played James Bond on the screen to date: Sean Connery, George Lazenby, Roger Moore, Timothy Dalton, and Pierce Brosnan.

This book is a celebration of the Bond legacy and should prove to be a suitable challenge for armchair secret agents the world over. Questions are designed to appeal to casual fans of the Bond films as well as die-hard aficionados who pride themselves on knowing every "top secret" bit of trivia associated with the movies. However, anyone who can answer more than 98 percent of the questions correctly should not only treat themselves to a martini (shaken, not stirred, of course) but also seriously consider getting out a bit more! Good hunting!

Acknowledgments

The author gratefully acknowledges the following sources for photos: World Wide, U.P.I., the British Film Institute, Columbia Pictures, Warner Brothers, and Jerry Ohlinger's Movie Memorabilia Store in New York City. Thanks also to everyone from Carol Publishing and Citadel Press: Steve Schragis, Gary Fitzgerald, Don Davidson, Colette Russen, and cover designer Steve Brower, and the many Bond fans from whom I solicited appropriate questions, especially Jason Allentoff and Joe Stechler. Among the books which were particularly helpful in researching this volume, I would like to specifically cite *The Incredible World of 007: An Authorized Celebration of James Bond* (1995, Citadel Press) by Lee Pfeiffer and Philip Lisa, the definitive authorized 007 story behind the making of the Bond films, and *The James Bond Encyclopedia* (1995, Contemporary Books) by Steven J. Rubin, an A-to-Z listing of virtually everything connected to the world of Mr. Kiss-Kiss-Bang-Bang.

The Ultimate James Bond Trivia Book

James Bond Trivia Questions

Dr. No

Dr. No, the first James Bond film, premiered in 1962. Although it was shot on a modest budget of $1 million, only producers Albert R. Broccoli and Harry Saltzman felt they had a hit on their hands. United Artists, the distributor, did not know what to make of the offbeat adventure which mixed violence, humor, and overt sexuality. Upon its release, however, audiences reacted fanatically to this new antihero, and a screen legend was born. For many, *Dr. No* is the quintessential Bond film. Here, 007 is very much an old-fashioned spy-detective who must rely on his instincts and training to survive. Subsequent films would see Bond aided by an increasingly fantastic arsenal of hi-tech gadgetry. Sean Connery was a virtual unknown when he was cast as Bond, but all of that would change practically overnight. Under the direction of Terence Young, Connery—a working-class actor with no exposure to the upper-crust world of Bond—would play the role so convincingly that he would be forever identified with Agent 007. *Dr. No* gave us any number of memorable scenes, villains, and performances, with Ursula Andress's first entrance in a white bikini as Honey Rider and Joseph Wiseman's menacing interpretation of the title character true classics.

Q1. Who tries to kill Bond by placing a tarantula in his bed?

Q2. Name the actor who portrays him.

Q3. How did Honey get revenge on the man who raped her?

Q4. From what Chinese crime syndicate did Dr. No defect?

Q5. What is the name of the character who gives Bond his new Walther PPK pistol? (He would later be known as "Q.")

Q6. Who plays him?

Q7. *Dr. No* is one of the two Bond films in which Desmond Llewelyn, who would play "Q," does not appear. Name the other from which he is absent.

Q8. What is the name of the British Secret Service agent murdered by the three blind men?

Q9. What is his secretary's name?

Q10. Who plays Miss Taro?

Q11. In which other Bond film does Eunice Gayson appear as Sylvia Trench, Bond's frustrated, would-be lover?

Q12. What song is Honey singing when she encounters Bond on the beach?

Q13. Where is Dr. No's island fortress located?

Q14. The actor seen in the famous gun-barrel opening of the first three Bond films is not Sean Connery. Can you name him?

Q15. Name the person who refused Ian Fleming's request to play Dr. No by responding in a telegram to the author, "No! No! No!"

Questions

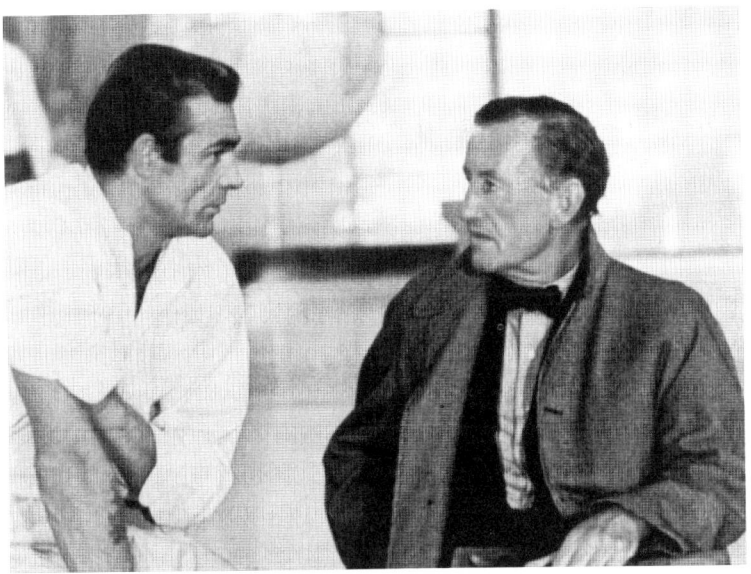

Ian Fleming chats with Sean Connery on the set of *Dr. No*

Q16. What does S.P.E.C.T.R.E. stand for?

Q17. Name of the owner of the restaurant where Bond tangles with Quarrel.

Q18. Who designed the main titles for *Dr. No*?

Q19. What is the name of the Dr. No henchman who poses as a chauffeur to deceive Bond?

Q20. Which gun does Bond have to surrender when his superior "M" insists he start using a Walther PPK?

Q21. What unusual physical characteristic does Dr. No have?

Q22. Who is the innovative film editor for *Dr. No* and the early Bond films? (He would also direct *On Her Majesty's Secret Service*.)

Q23. What is the name of Bond's C.I.A. contact in Jamaica?

Q24. Who plays him?

Q25. Who is credited with composing the James Bond theme?

From Russia With Love

Even Broccoli and Saltzman confessed to being surprised at the magnitude of the public response to 007. They ensured fans that the follow-up film, *From Russia With Love,* would be even more exotic. For his sophomore appearance as Bond, Sean Connery was assisted by Daniela Bianchi as the love interest, Lotte Lenya and Robert Shaw as two of the series' best villains, and Terence Young's outstanding direction. *From Russia With Love* followed Fleming's source novel quite closely, although several action highlights were embellished for the big screen. Among the memorable sequences: Bond being stalked by Robert Shaw as Red Grant in the pre-credits sequence; the spectacular destruction of the S.P.E.C.T.R.E. motorboat fleet; Bond being hunted by an enemy helicopter, and the brutal fist fight between Bond and Grant on the Orient Express. Released in early 1964, *From Russia With Love* remains Sean Connery's personal favorite among the Bond movies.

Q26. Name is the actor who plays S.P.E.C.T.R.E. villain Morzeny. (He would go on to play General Gogol in future films.)

Q27. What actress plays the masseuse on S.P.E.C.T.R.E. island?

Q28. Where were the sequences of S.P.E.C.T.R.E. island shot?

Q29. Name the two actresses who play the battling gypsy girls?

Q30. How long does it take for Grant to kill Bond's double in the pre-credit sequence?

Q31. What type of fish does Blofeld keep in his office?

Q32. What number does Lotte Lenya as Rosa Klebb hold in the S.P.E.C.T.R.E. organization?

Q33. What number does Kronsteen (Vladek Sheybal) hold?

Q34. Name the chess player whom Kronsteen defeats.

Q35. How many gold sovereigns does Bond's attaché case contain?

Q36. What is the cover for Kerim Bey's (Pedro Armendariz) Istanbul office?

Q37. What was Bey's former profession?

Q38. What reason does Bond use to request another hotel room when he discovers his is "bugged"?

Q39. Name the Soviet assassin Kerim Bey kills with a sniper's rifle?

Q40. What other film produced by Broccoli and Saltzman is "plugged" in *From Russia With Love*?

Q41. What aliases do Bond and Tatiana (Daniela Bianchi) assume on the Orient Express?

Q42. What is the name of the enemy agent whom Bond and Bey capture on the train?

Q43. Name the British agent Grant kills at the train station.

Q44. What does Grant order for dinner aboard the train?

Q45. How long does it take for the poisonous venom to kill Kronsteen?

Q46. Where are Bond and Tatiana heading in their speedboat?

Q47. What cast member's name is misspelled in the main title credits?

Q48. Who plays the belly dancer at the gypsy camp?

Q49. How many lovers prior to Bond has Tatiana admitted to having?

Q50. Who sings the film's title song and who wrote it?

Goldfinger

For many, *Goldfinger* represents the high-water mark for the Bond series—for it was in this third 007 epic that the film truly capitalized on humor. The first two Bonds were rather somber, and following *Goldfinger* they would become—with rare exceptions—increasingly "over the top" in terms of the wisecracks and gags. With *Goldfinger,* the balance was just about perfect, and Guy Hamilton—taking over the director's chair from Terence Young—deserved much of the credit. The film had a budget that was as large as the first two Bonds combined, and it was spent wisely by the producers. *Goldfinger* looks gargantuan in size, when in reality much of it was shot on the backlot. With this movie,

Questions

Sean Connery and Honor Blackman on the set of *Goldfinger*

Agent 007 became an absolute phenomenon, and with the outstanding response to the introduction of the fabulous Aston Martin DB5, the gadgets from "Q" Branch were here to stay—for better or worse.

Q51. What is the license plate number of Bond's Aston Martin DB5?

Q52. For which nations does the car carry license plates?

Q53. What is the code name for Gert Frobe as Goldfinger's plan to destroy Fort Knox?

Q54. Name the gangster crushed by Harold Sakata as Oddjob in the limousine.

Q55. Who played Tilly Masterson?

Q56. What type of car did Oddjob chauffeur for Goldfinger?

Q57. Name the actor who plays the thug Bond electrocutes in the bathtub.

Q58. What does Bond toss into the tub to cause the shock of the guy's life?

Q59. In what city does Bond first meet Goldfinger?

Q60. What is Goldfinger's first name?

Q61. What does Bond say when he hears "My name is Pussy Galore," purred by Honor Blackman?

Q62. What type of golf ball does Goldfinger play?

Q63. What is the name of the nerve gas Goldfinger plans to spray on the troops at Fort Knox?

Q64. How many seconds are left when the atomic bomb is disarmed?

Q65. Who is the Red Chinese man who gives Goldfinger the nuclear bomb?

Q66. Burt Kwouk played the Red Chinese man. For what other role is he primarily known?

Q67. What type of vehicle conceals the laser beam in the assault on Fort Knox?

Q68. What type of drink does Bond share with Goldfinger at the stud farm?

Q69. Where is the stud farm located?

Q70. Who plays Kisch?

Q71. Name the actor who plays Felix Leiter.

Q72. *Goldfinger* won an Oscar in what category?

Q73. What device on the Aston Martin does "Q" demonstrate, but Bond is not seen using?

Q74. What other Bond film is seen in the opening credits?

Thunderball

Thunderball was a troubled film to get off the ground. Production had been delayed for several years due to a lawsuit among writers Kevin McClory and Jack Whittingham and Ian Fleming. Fleming had worked on a screenplay about Bond with these men years earlier. When the project fell through, Fleming borrowed elements of the script and used them as the basis for his novel, *Thunderball*. The resulting plagiarism suit not only was embarrassing to Fleming, but it also delayed production of the movie version of *Thunderball* until after his death. In addition the suit awarded McClory screen rights to the novel. McClory ended up producing the 1965 film version in conjunction with Broccoli and Saltzman. What turned out was an epic movie in every way, and at $6 million the most expensive Bond made to that time. The film was truly a spectacle and became the movie event of the year. Before long, Bond merchandise mania had spread worldwide. Yet, not everything was blissful. Director Terence Young—back for the third time—dismissed the movie as too slow moving; some critics complained that the hardware and gadgetry now overshadowed the characters; Broccoli and Saltzman's fragile partnership was becoming more strained, and Sean Connery griped that he disliked being the focus of Bond mania and was counting the days until he could leave the series. Nevertheless, *Thunderball* was—and is—a remarkable adventure.

Q75. What two actors play the widow in the pre-credits sequence?

Q76. What is Fiona's (Luciana Paluzzi) last name?

Q77. With what does Largo (Adolfo Celi) intend to torture Domino (Claudine Auger)?

Q78. Who frees Domino aboard the *Disco Volante*?

Q79. For what did *Thunderball* win an Oscar?

Q80. Who played Vargas?

Q81. Name the restaurant where Bond and Domino dine and dance.

Q82. In the pre-credits scene, what enemy assassin's funeral does Bond attend?

Q83. Who plays Felix Leiter?

Q84. What is the name of Largo's estate?

Q85. In what city is S.P.E.C.T.R.E. headquarters located?

Q86. What insignia is on the S.P.E.C.T.R.E. ring?

Q87. What S.P.E.C.T.R.E. agent is killed by rockets fired from Fiona's motorcycle?

Q88. Name the health clinic to which Bond is assigned.

Q89. What device does Bond use to lock Lippe in the steam cabinet?

Q90. Who played Pat Fearing, Bond's paramour with a penchant for mink gloves?

Q91. What city is the target of the S.P.E.C.T.R.E. nuclear assault?

Q92. What is the maximum time Bond's underwater breather is operable?

Q93. Name the NATO officer who is killed by Fiona and Lippe.

Q94. What type of NATO aircraft is hijacked?

Q95. What is the name of the club in which Fiona is killed?

Q96. Who rescues Bond from the cave?

Q97. What witticism does Bond remark upon killing Vargas with a speargun?

Q98. Name the character played by Martine Beswick.

Q99. Who sings the film's title song?

Casino Royale

By 1967, the James Bond phenomenon had grown to monumental proportions and virtually every producer in Hollywood was eager to jump on the "Bondwagon." Broccoli and

Saltzman owned the screen rights to all of Ian Fleming's James Bond novels, except one: *Casino Royale*. This had been the first of the 007 thrillers, and as it was originally met with apathy by an unresponsive public when it was published in 1953, Ian Fleming immediately had sold the screen rights to gain some short-term cash. Although he quickly showed more confidence in his creation and would guard the rights to all future Bond novels until the Broccoli-Saltzman deal, the fact was that the future of *Casino Royale* remained outside of Fleming's control. A "quickie" 1954 one-hour live TV adaptation of the book had been broadcast by CBS on its *Climax!* series. By 1966, producer Charles K. Feldman secured the *Casino* rights and attempted to lure Sean Connery into starring in a big screen version. Tired of Bond and under exclusive contract to Broccoli and Saltzman, Connery declined.

Feldman then made a bizarre decision: Rather than compete with Connery at the box office with a straight Bond film starring another actor, he announced *Casino Royale* would be a spectacular satire starring a veritable "Who's Who" of the international cinema. This glorious mess would ultimately consume many millions of dollars, as well as the efforts of five directors. There is nary a resemblance to Fleming's excellent source novel, and the movie makes *It's a Mad, Mad, Mad, Mad World* look positively subdued by comparison.

Contrary to popular belief, however, *Casino Royale* (released in the summer of 1967) drew very large audiences and some surprisingly enthusiastic reviews. Nevertheless, the out-of-control production cost insured the movie would lose money, and it is not regarded fondly by most Bond fans. As failures go, however, it remains an interesting and often highly entertaining one.

Questions

Q100. Who plays Jimmy Bond?

Q101. What former Bond leading lady is also the leading lady in *Casino Royale*?

Q102. Who performed the title song?

Q103. What song from the film was nominated for an Oscar?

Q104. What popular actor makes a cameo appearance dressed as a Scottish bagpipe player?

Q105. It took five directors to bring this film to the screen. Name them.

Q106. Who plays agent Cooper, later to disguise himself as James Bond?

Q107. What is the name of the character played by William Holden?

Q108. What does Lady Fiona refer to her late husband's toupee as?

Q109. Name two actors from *From Russia With Love* and *Goldfinger* who appear in *Casino Royale*?

Q110. What is the name of Peter Sellers's character?

Q111. What role does Jacqueline Bisset play?

Q112. Who plays Moneypenny's daughter?

Q113. Orson Welles plays the villainous Le Chiffre. Who played the role in the 1954 live TV version of the novel?

Q114. What Oscar-winning song by John Barry is heard in the film?

Ursula Andress and Peter Sellers in the bizarre big-screen adaptation of *Casino Royale*

Q115. What rare flower does David Niven as Sir James Bond proudly show off in his garden?

Q116. What is Jimmy Bond's evil alias?

Q117. Which famous actor announces that he has just shot himself with a trick gun during the climactic casino brawl?

Q118. With whom did Sir James Bond sire a daughter out of wedlock?

Q119. For what organization does Le Chiffre work?

Q120. What diabolical scheme does Dr. Noah intend to carry out?

Q121. Who composed the musical score?

Q122. Who plays "M"?

Q123. What physical handicap does Jimmy Bond develop in the presence of his uncle, Sir James Bond?

Q124. From what speech impediment does Sir James Bond suffer?

You Only Live Twice

You Only Live Twice marked Sean Connery's fifth appearance as James Bond, and it was a tired, exasperated actor who reluctantly went before the cameras for this hi-tech adventure. The film was shot largely in Japan, and Connery was shocked at the habits of the generally subdued Japanese paparazzi. He became the centerpiece of fanatical press coverage that even extended to his being followed into bathrooms. Midway through production, Connery became so irritable that Broccoli and Saltzman allowed him to resign from the series despite the fact that he was contractually obligated to do one more Bond film.

Twice is filled with eye-popping set-pieces and extravagant action sequences. However, the increasing amount of hi-tech equipment came at the expense of characterizations. Connery griped that the hardware insured that the production schedules became longer and increasingly unpredictable, as well as a negative influence on the character of

Bond. Critics agreed that with *Twice*—an admittedly superb action film—Bond was less a detective than the caretaker of "Q's" amazing arsenal. The movie opened in the summer of 1967, in direct competition with *Casino Royale*. The Connery film easily outgrossed its rival and became a major hit—although grosses were considerably less than those for *Thunderball*. Connery announced with relief that he was saying good riddance to the role that had admittedly made him a star, but which had become "a Frankenstein monster." He was off to Spain to film the Western *Shalako* with Brigitte Bardot. Broccoli and Saltzman then had to find someone talented enough—or crazy enough—to fill Sean Connery's shoes as Agent 007.

Q125. What popular author of children's books wrote the screenplay?

Q126. Who played Aki?

Q127. How many times is Kissy Suzuki referred to by name?

Q128. Who is Bond's intelligence contact in Tokyo?

Q129. Who plays Blofeld?

Q130. Who plays Kissy?

Q131. Who is the head of the Japanese Secret Service?

Q132. What are the code words Miss Moneypenny (Lois Maxwell) tells Bond he must remember?

Q133. What is the name of the cargo ship Bond investigates on the Kobe docks?

Q134. Who is the industrial tycoon who secretly works for S.P.E.C.T.R.E.?

Q135. Who is his "confidential secretary?"

Questions

Q136. What happens to her?

Q137. Where is "M's" office located in Japan?

Q138. Where are Blofeld's headquarters hidden?

Q139. What is the name of Blofeld's Aryan henchman in the control room?

Q140. Who is the production designer for the film?

Q141. In what city is Bond "assassinated" in the pre-credits scene?

Q142. Who is Bond's lover in the pre-credits scene?

Q143. How does Bond disguise himself to investigate S.P.E.C.T.R.E. activities on a small Japanese island?

Q144. What type of deterrent does Bond find in the cave leading to the S.P.E.C.T.R.E. volcano?

Q145. How many seconds are left to spare when Bond stops the countdown to World War III?

Q146. Who or what is Little Nellie?

Q147. What type of car does Bond drive in the film?

Q148. How does Tanaka describe the physical appearance of Bond's unseen bride-to-be?

Q149. Who sings the film's title song?

On Her Majesty's Secret Service

A worldwide talent hunt was launched to find the new James Bond. Meanwhile, George Lazenby, an Australian male model with no acting experience, had devised a scheme to land the role of the century. He arrived in London filled with self-confidence that he could bluff Broccoli and Saltzman into hiring him by pretending to be an experienced actor. The ruse worked—the producers were immediately impressed, as was the director. Lazenby defied all the odds and overnight became the center of an international publicity campaign.

George Lanzenby enjoys some Bondian perks in *On Her Majesty's Secret Service*

Lazenby's debut as 007 would be the 1969 Christmas release, *On Her Majesty's Secret Service*—one of Fleming's best novels. It was boldly decided to forgo the hi-tech gadgetry and concentrate on making this a realistic love story and adventure film. By all accounts, *OHMSS* succeeded on every level. However, midway through production, Lazenby fell under the influence of "know-it-alls" who assured him Bond would not last into the 1970s because it was an outdated concept in the era of hippies. He was convinced to reject the producers' requests to sign a five-picture deal. Instead, he quit the role of Bond. Lazenby would soon learn that he had few opportunities to find stardom. His reputation as being difficult effectively blackballed him from major parts.

Ironically, while *OHMSS* was underrated at the time of its release, and grossed far less than the previous Bonds, both Lazenby and the movie are today held in high regard, with many fans considering it the best film of the series. Lazenby went on to success with financial investments and continues to act in supporting roles. He candidly admits his decision to abandon Bond was "stupid," but he is justifiably proud of his lasting contribution to the series.

Q150. What is the name of Blofeld's (Telly Savalas) institute for research on allergies?

Q151. What objects from previous films does Bond take from his desk drawer?

Q152. What two actresses in this film appeared in *The Avengers* TV series?

Q153. Name Blofeld's female "right-hand man."

Q154. What alias does Bond use to infiltrate Blofeld's compound?

Q155. What is the Bond family crest motto?

Q156. What is the name of Tracy's father?

Q157. What is the bizarre physical characteristic of the Blofelds?

Q158. What does Bond use to sneak out of his locked room at Piz Gloria?

Q159. How much does Tracy's father offer Bond to marry his daughter?

Q160. What memento does Bond give to Moneypenny (Lois Maxwell) at his wedding?

Q161. In which country do Bond and Tracy marry?

Q162. What is "M's" hobby?

Q163. What is the name of the agent killed atop Piz Gloria by Blofeld's men as he attempts to scale the mountain?

Q164. What former Bond editor made his directorial debut with *OHMSS*?

Q165. When his captors bring him to Draco's office, Bond hears a theme song from a previous film. What is the song and the context in which he hears it?

Q166. How does Ruby (Angela Scoular) inform Bond of her room number as they dine at Piz Gloria?

Q167. Whom does Bond toast after resigning from the secret service?

Q168. What is the only gadget introduced by "Q" (Desmond Llewelyn) in the film?

Q169. What is the main element of the Blofeld coat of arms?

Questions 21

George Lazenby's Bond flirts with Lois Maxwell's Moneypenny in *On Her Majesty's Secret Service*

Q170. Who assassinates Tracy?

Q171. What is the name of the love song played during the film?

Q172. Who sings it?

Q173. What car does Bond drive in the pre-credits scene?

Q174. What is the last line of dialogue in the film?

Diamonds Are Forever

With George Lazenby having resigned as 007, Broccoli and Saltzman had the challenge of finding the third Bond actor in as many years for the next film, *Diamonds Are Forever,* set to be a Christmas 1971 release. Numerous overtures were made to an uninterested Sean Connery, until he was finally made an offer he couldn't refuse: the highest salary ever paid to an actor at that time. Connery agreed to a one-shot return as Bond because he needed the salary to start a charity in his native Scotland. He might have also been frustrated by the failure of his recent non-Bondian efforts.

Diamonds Are Forever is rather a lame affair when contrasted with the earlier films, and perhaps due to the soft grosses of *OHMSS,* the producers unwisely chose to go back to the hi-tech atmosphere—only this time with outrageous humor instead of subtle wisecracks. While second-rate Bond, the film generated enormous business and proved to the world that the franchise was alive and well. Connery, however, resigned for good, and Broccoli and Saltzman had to prove that there was life in the franchise *without* Sean Connery.

Q175. Bloefeld here is played by Charles Gray. In what previous Bond film did he appear?

Q176. What is the name of the diamond smuggler Bond impersonates?

Q177. Who plays the real Peter Franks?

Q178. How is Moneypenny disguised when she meets Bond?

Q179. Who plays the gangster who tells Bond, "I didn't know there was a pool down there," upon throwing Plenty O'Toole (Lana Wood) from the window?

Questions

Q180. Willard Whyte is played by what multitalent?

Q181. Who plays Mr. Wint and who plays Mr. Kidd?

Q182. What type of car does Tiffany Case (Jill St. John) drive?

Q183. Who plays Bert Saxby?

Q184. What is the name of the technician Bond impersonates to investigate Willard Whyte's space facility in the desert?

Q185. Who is the Dutch schoolteacher who secretly works for S.P.E.C.T.R.E.?

Q186. Who sings the title song?

Q187. What is the name of the hotel Willard Whyte owns?

Q188. Who are Bambi and Thumper?

Q189. How does Bond smuggle the diamonds from Amsterdam into the U.S.?

Q190. What is the name of the elderly nightclub comedian murdered by Wint and Kidd?

Q191. Who plays him?

Q192. When Bond's buxom admirer, Ms. O'Toole, introduces herself by saying, "Hi, I'm Plenty!" how does 007 respond?

Q193. What is the name of the woman Bond threatens to strangle in the pre-credits sequence?

Q194. As Bond soaks in a club inside his suite in the casino, he reads an entertainment magazine. What performer is on the cover?

Q195. In what vehicle does Blofeld attempt to escape the oil rig?

Q196. Where is the rig located?

Q197. Whose voice does Bond imitate when speaking with Blofeld over the phone?

Q198. Who is the man with "M" who gives Bond the details of the diamond smuggling operation?

Q199. What is the name of the dentist whom Wint and Kidd kill with a scorpion?

Sean Connery and director Guy Hamilton "take five" on the set of *Diamonds Are Forever* in Las Vegas

Live and Let Die

In their new search for the next James Bond, the producers decided to go with an established name. That person turned out to be Roger Moore, the popular TV star who had also created a legendary espionage screen persona with his interpretation of "The Saint." Unlike Connery, Moore specialized in broad humor, and never took the plots very seriously. With his debut in the 1973 Bond thriller *Live and Let Die,* he proved to be controversial among Bond fans. Some felt he was too pretty and flippant in the role, while others thought he brought a refreshing presence to the series. For better or worse, everyone agreed that Moore established his own interpretation of James Bond. The public showed its support by making *Live and Let Die* a major hit—although not quite of the Connery proportions. A new era for 007 was about to begin and Roger Moore would increasingly win over most of his most vocal critics.

Q200. Who is Dr. Kananga's (Yaphet Kotto) alter ego in the Harlem drug trade?

Q201. On what Caribbean island does Kananga operate?

Q202. What is the name of Kananga's obese henchman with the raspy voice?

Q203. How does Bond render Tee-Hee's (Julius Harris) mechanical arm useless in the fight aboard the train?

Q204. What Academy Award nomination did the film receive?

Q205. What former Beatles associate composed the musical score?

Q206. How does Solitaire (Jane Seymour) lose the ability to foretell the future?

Q207. What is the name of Sheriff Pepper's (Clifton James) brother-in-law?

Q208. What famous actor-dancer played Baron Samedi?

Q209. Name the British agent whose death Bond is investigating.

Q210. What gadget from "Q" branch fails to save Bond when he is threatened by alligators?

Q211. Who is the hapless lady to whom Bond gives "flying lessons?"

Q212. What is the restaurant chain which acts as a cover for Kananga's operations?

Q213. What test does Kananga give Solitaire to see if she has lost her powers to predict the future?

Q214. Who plays Rosie Carver?

Q215. When visiting Bond's apartment, "M" watches 007 operate a seemingly complicated machine, and then asks, "Is that all it does?" What was he referring to?

Q216. Who pilots the boat which takes Bond and Rosie fishing?

Q217. In which previous 007 film did we also see Bond's apartment?

Q218. What voodoo warning does Rosie find in Bond's hotel room?

Q219. What are the two methods of rendering an alligator helpless which Tee-Hee shares with Bond?

Q220. What is the name of the alligator who bit off Tee-Hee's arm?

Questions

Q221. In what other Bond film does Sheriff Pepper appear?

Q222. What is the name of Bond's C.I.A. contact in Harlem?

Q223. What is the name of the Italian agent Bond beds in the pre-credits scene?

Q224. Who wrote the screenplay?

The Man With the Golden Gun

Roger Moore's second outing as Agent 007 was a weak, uninspired film based on one of Fleming's least inspired novels (albeit the last full-length 007 thriller he would ever write). *The Man With the Golden Gun* was so filled with juvenile sight gags and ludicrous plot gimmicks (i.e., a villainous midget and a ridiculous Kung-Fu fight in which Bond is saved by two teenage girls who can outfight him) that even the most die-hard fans felt the series had probably run out of steam. Box-office grosses were considerably less than Moore's previous outing, and the understanding seemed to be that if he and the producers could not come up with something better than this, it was time for Agent 007 to finally resign from Her Majesty's cinematic secret service.

Q225. Name the Oriental beauty whom Bond encounters in a swimming pool?

Q226. What ritual does archvillain Scaramanga (Christopher Lee) practice prior to performing an assassination?

Q227. Maud Adams plays Andrea. In what other Bond film does she star?

Q228. Other than those at MI 5, who repeats his role from the previous 007 movie?

Q229. What is the name of the nightclub where Scaramanga does away with the British solar energy expert?

Q230. What is the solar energy expert's name?

Q231. Who plays the millionaire Hai Fat?

Q232. Which partially sunken ocean liner serves as the secret headquarters of British intelligence in Hong Kong?

Q233. Who sings the film's title song?

Q234. In which other film does the ill-fated gangster in the pre-credits sequence appear?

Q235. While in Hong Kong, Sheriff Pepper is inexplicably looking to purchase a car. What make and model automobile is he about to test when Bond jumps in and takes him on the ride of his life?

Q236. Who is Scaramanga's midget henchman?

Q237. Who plays him?

Q238. Whom does Britt Eklund play?

Q239. What is the name of the Secret Service agent Bond works with in Hong Kong?

Q240. How much does Scaramanga charge to perform a "hit?"

Q241. What peculiar physical characteristic does Scaramanga have?

Q242. As what does Scaramanga disguise his deadly obstacle course?

Questions

Roger Moore on the set of *The Man With the Golden Gun*

Q243. On what type of vessel do Bond and Mary Goodnight escape Scaramanga's island?

Q244. Bond is investigating the murder of agent Bill Fairbanks. What was Fairbanks's double-0 number?

Q245. Where does Bond find the bullet which killed Fairbanks?

Q246. After escaping from the Kung Fu school, Bond gets some unexpected support in his battle with his pursuers. Who comes to his aid?

Q247. In what month and year was the film released in the United States?

Q248. This was the fourth Bond film Guy Hamilton directed for Broccoli and Saltzman. Which big-budget war epic did he direct for Harry Saltzman in 1969?

Q249. Who composed the score for the film?

The Spy Who Loved Me

As James Bond for the third time, Roger Moore not only rescued his reputation as an actor, but also insured that the series came back in a spectacular fashion. The long production delay between the release of *Golden Gun* and the premiere of *The Spy Who Loved Me* in 1977 was due to the split up of Broccoli and Saltzman's tenuous partnership (Cubby would now produce the films alone) and to the fact that this movie was so epic in scope that the largest soundstage in the world had to be constructed at Pinewood Studios. *The Spy Who Loved Me* would be the biggest

Roger Moore and Barbara Bach at a press conference for *The Spy Who Loved Me*

budgeted Bond yet, and one of the most entertaining. With all the elements finally jelling right, Roger Moore was able to make Bond every bit his own. Audiences and critics agreed, and despite the summer of 1977 belonging to *Star Wars*, *Spy* also became an international box-office sensation, as well as a suprising critical success.

Q250. Name the three Oscar nominations the film received.

Q251. Who plays the part of the U.S. submarine captain?

Q252. What unique physical characteristic does Stromberg (Curt Jurgens) have?

Q253. Who is the bald villain whom Bond allows to plummet to his death from a rooftop?

Q254. Name the man whom Jaws (Richard Kiel) kills inside an Egyptian pyramid.

Q255. What is Anya's (Barbara Bach) code name in the Soviet Secret Service?

Q256. What is the name of Anya's fiancée whom Bond kills in the pre-credits sequence?

Q257. Who is the curvaceous henchwoman of Stromberg's who attempts to kill Bond and Anya in a helicopter attack?

Q258. Who plays her?

Q259. Who is the stuntman who performs the famed ski jump in the pre-credits scene?

Q260. Who plays the Minister of Defense?

Q261. What rank does Bond hold in the Royal Navy?

Q262. What is the name of Stromberg's tanker?

Q263. What is the name of Stromberg's underwater city?

Q264. What type of car does Bond receive from "Q" Branch?

Q265. What is the license plate of the car?

Q266. How does "M" contact 007 in the pre-credits scene?

Q267. What device does Bond utilize on his car to thwart Jaws's pursuing vehicle?

Q268. What character does Jaws kill at the Cairo's Mojaba nightclub?

Q269. Robert Brown, who would go on to play "M," has what role in this film?

Q270. When Bond and Anya are caught coitus-interuptus by "M" and the government brass, what does Bond say he is doing (it's the final line in the film)?

Questions

Roger Moore in *The Spy Who Loved Me*

Q271. Who wrote the film's musical score?

Q272. Whos sings the title song?

Q273. Which Bond film was originally slated to follow *The Spy Who Loved Me*?

Moonraker

The expression "bigger is not necessarily better" fully describes *Moonraker*, a colossal production that would make *The Spy Who Loved Me* seem like a low-budget film. As his second solo effort producing the Bond films, Cubby Broccoli certainly didn't stint on the money or the talent. However, this out-of-space yarn rivals *Golden Gun* as the silliest film in the series. While impressive to look at, the overabundance of juvenile humor alienated die-hard fans (although critics seemed to love the slapstick). The film, released in the summer of 1979, was the largest grossing Bond epic to date, but Broccoli knew that carrying Bond into outerspace was as far as he could go in terms of sacrificing any semblance of realism. Despite the overwhelming box-office success of *Moonraker*, Cubby heeded the criticisms of the fans and decided it was time to bring Bond back down to earth.

Q274. Who plays the villainous Hugo Drax?

Q275. Who is Drax's Oriental henchman?

Q276. In what city does Bond discover a glass factory being used as a front for Drax's covert activities?

Q277. Who plays Holly Goodhead?

Questions

Q278. When Bond compliments Holly on her fighting skills, he inquires if she learned them at NASA. In fact, where does she tell him she learned her adeptness at self-defense?

Q279. The film received an Oscar nomination in what category?

Q280. Who sings the title song?

Q281. Over what geographical area does the Moonraker disappear in the pre-credits scene?

Q282. In the pre-credits scene, Bond is aboard a small jet wherein he has a struggle with two enemy agents. What is the name of the airline?

Q283. What is the minister of defense's name?

Q284. Where is Drax's manufacturing facility for the Moonraker shuttles?

Q285. What is the name of Drax's manservant, who introduces Bond to his boss?

Q286. Who are the two women for whom Drax is playing a piano concerto?

Q287. What is England's "one indisputable contribution to western civilization," according to Drax?

Q288. When entering the centrifuge, Bond is warned that a certain number of "G's" are fatal. What is the number?

Q289. Who plays Corinne Dufour?

Q290. What is the name of Jaws's (Richard Kiel) girlfriend?

Q291. What is Jaws's only line of dialogue in his two Bond films?

Q292. What is the name of the glass factory Bond investigates in Italy?

Q293. What famous theme from a Steven Spielberg film is heard in *Moonraker*?

Q294. What theme from a classic Western is heard as Bond is seen riding as a caballero?

Q295. What brand and year of champagne do Bond and Holly share in her hotel room?

Q296. Bond's contact in Rio is Manuela. Who plays her?

Q297. Where are British Intelligence headquarters located in Rio?

Q298. Where does Holly conceal a flamethrower?

For Your Eyes Only

The title *For Your Eyes Only* is from a book of short stories by Ian Fleming. There is virtually no resemblance to those stories in this film which bears the book's name, but there is plenty to recommend here. Although *FYEO* still has some ill-conceived silliness, the last hour adds up to what is among the best Bond stories ever brought to the screen. The gadgetry was minimized, and Roger Moore was actually given some dramatic situations and dialogue to work with. The film boasts what was arguably his best performance as 007. The tale of revenge and international intrigue was also refreshingly realistic, much to the delight of the Bond faithful who praised the filmmakers for bringing Bond back to his roots—at least relative to *Moonraker*.

Questions

Q299. Who is the villain in the pre-credits sequence trying to kill Bond by trapping him aboard a helicopter?

Q300. What Oscar nomination did the film receive?

Q301. Who wrote the musical score?

Q302. Who sings the title song?

Q303. What character does ice skater Lynn Holly-Johnson play?

Q304. Who plays Columbo?

Q305. Who is the assassin who kills Melina Havelock's (Carole Bouquet) parents?

Q306. Which veteran of the Bond team made his debut as director with this film?

Q307. In "M's" absence, who assigns Bond to his latest mission?

Q308. The actress who plays Countess Lisl would eventually wed a James Bond actor. What is her name and whom did she marry?

Q309. What is Greek millionaire Kristatos's first name?

Q310. Who plays him?

Q311. Who is the assassin whom Bond allows to plummet over the side of a cliff in a car?

Q312. What prominent British politician is seen at the end of the film and who portrays this person?

Q313. What is the name of Melina's talking parrot?

Q314. Where is Bond first seen in the pre-credits sequence?

Q315. What is the name of the ship which sinks when it hits a mine?

Q316. What is the device which Bond is trying to recover?

Q317. Who is Bond's contact in Italy?

Q318. The film is based in part on Ian Fleming's short story of the same name. What other short story was adapted for the screenplay?

Q319. The sequence in which Bond and Melina are "keel-hauled" through shark infested waters actually appears in a different 007 novel. Which one?

Q320. What is the nickname of Columbo?

Q321. Where does Kristatos maintain a headquarters while awaiting the arrival of General Gogol (Walter Gotell)?

Q322. Who plays Jacoba Brink, the skating coach?

Octopussy

Octopussy returns 007 to the spectacle of the earlier films, and ignores the much heralded realism of *For Your Eyes Only*. Fortunately, despite plenty of opportunity for ridiculousness, the script never goes so over the top that it detracts from what is basically a very involving storyline. Roger Moore was by this time so comfortable in the role that even he could joke that his emotions consisted of raising either one or both eyebrows. Nevertheless, this Bond epic, set in India amid some stunning locations, boasts some incredible action sequences and an excellent cast. *Octopussy*

Questions

was a huge commercial hit upon its release in 1983, although Roger Moore repeated his oft-stated vow that he was retiring from the role.

Q323. What popular Indian-born tennis pro costars as Bond's ally?

Q324. What is the title of the main theme song?

Q325. Who sings it?

Q326. Name the mad Soviet general played by Steven Berkoff?

Q327. In this film, Miss Moneypenny has a young assistant. What is her name?

Q328. Who designed and flew the Acrostar mini-jet used in the pre-credits sequence?

Q329. Who is the villain played by Louis Jourdan?

Q330. The auction of the Fabergé egg is based upon a Bond short story. Which one?

Q331. In the pre-credits sequence, a British agent disguised as a clown is murdered. What was his double-0 number?

Q332. What is the name of Octopussy's (Maud Adams) elaborate home?

Q333. What is Octopussy's means of transportation on the water?

Q334. What is the name of Octopussy's "right-hand woman," played by Kristina Wayborn?

Q335. What does Bond use to knock Gobinda (Kabir Bedi) off the top of the jet on which they are struggling?

Q336. The James Bond theme is played by someone in a crowd scene in the film. In what context is it heard?

Q337. What deadly device almost kills Bond while he is in bed with Octopussy?

Q338. What is the name of the army officer Bond impersonates in the pre-credits scene?

Q339. What is Bond's mission code-named?

Q340. Bond defeats Kamal Khan with a roll of the villain's own "loaded" dice. What does 007 roll?

Q341. While a captive, Bond is invited to an exotic dinner by Kamal Khan and Octopussy. What revolting dish does Khan indulge in?

Q342. How does Bond disguise himself to infiltrate Octopussy's palace?

Q343. What tattoo does Magda sport on her back?

Q344. Who is the MI 5 art expert who accompanies Bond to the auction of the Fabergé egg?

Q345. Of what does the Fabergé egg contain a meticulously crafted replica?

Q346. What device from "Q Branch" does Bond use to escape his quarters at Octopussy's palace?

Q347. Name the real-life brothers who portray the evil knife-throwing twins who menace 007.

Never Say Never Again

The convoluted history of *Never Say Never Again* could fill volumes. Briefly, producer Kevin McClory was awarded the screen rights to *Thunderball* as part of the settlement of an early 1960s plagiarism suit against Ian Fleming. Although McClory coproduced the screen version of *Thunderball* in conjunction with Broccoli and Saltzman, he now wanted to recycle the property. After many aborted attempts to make a Bond film to rival Cubby Broccoli's, McClory joined forces with producer-attorney Jack Schwartzman and cleared numerous legal hurdles. Finally, a Bond film was in the works, and amazingly Schwartzman convinced Sean Connery to star. Connery said he was intrigued to play Bond one last time as an older man. Despite legal challenges by Broccoli, the film—a loose remake of *Thunderball*—was completed and released in the fall of 1983. Critics were kind to the offbeat Bond effort, with most enthusiastically praising Connery's world-weary performance as 007. However, *NSNA* was a troubled film, and many of the technical and artistic problems were apparent in the final cut. Still, it boasts one of Sean's best performances and some wonderful sequences that work better independently than the film does on the whole. Curiously, the much-heralded "Battle of the Bonds" for domination of the box office in 1983 turned out to be a non-event, with both *NSNA* and Roger Moore's *Octopussy* finding enormous success.

Q348. Who has the role of "M"?

Q349. Who plays Moneypenny this time around?

Q350. Name the character played by Barbara Carrera.

Q351. Where are the S.P.E.C.T.R.E. headquarters located?

Sean Connery and Kim Bassinger in *Never Say Never Again*, the "unofficial" remake of *Thunderball*

Questions

Q352. What legendary tale is depicted on the pendant which Largo (Klaus Maia Brandauer) gives to Domino (Kim Basinger)?

Q353. What is Largo's first name?

Q354. Who is number 12 in S.P.E.C.T.R.E.?

Q355. What is the name of Domino's doomed brother?

Q356. What does Bond throw in Lippe's (Pat Roach) face to immobilize him during the fight at Shrublands?

Q357. Who plays Blofeld?

Q358. Whose eye does S.P.E.C.T.R.E. have to replicate in order to activate the nuclear bombs?

Q359. What ransom does S.P.E.C.T.R.E. demand of each nation in exchange for not causing a nuclear holocaust?

Q360. Who plays "Q"?

Q361. In this film, "Q's" real name is not Boothroyd. What is it?

Q362. Popular British comedy star Rowan Atkinson has a supporting role as a bumbling agent. What is his character's name?

Q363. How many pounds does Bond tell "M" he lost during the Shrublands fight?

Q364. What former football star plays the role of Felix Leiter?

Q365. What is the name of the agent whose body Bond finds in his water bed?

Q366. What drink does Domino order when she is with Bond at the casino?

Q367. How much does Bond forfeit in cash winnings in return for a dance with Domino?

Q368. Who sings the title song?

Q369. How does Fatima kill Petachi?

Q370. Who composed the musical score for the film?

Q371. "Q" complains that without Bond in the field, things have gotten awfully dull around MI 5. What does he hope Bond brings back with him?

Q372. Who is the actress who fishes Bond out of the ocean?

A View to a Kill

Although Roger Moore insisted that *Octopussy* was his Bond swan song, Cubby Broccoli convinced him to make one more 007 epic: *A View to a Kill,* released in 1985. By all accounts, Moore had gone a film too far, looking more than a bit long in the tooth for the action sequences. *View* also took a direct turn back to the era of slapstick, making the last several Bond films wildly inconsistent in style. Embarrassing sight gags mar most of the story, although the last half hour is terrifically exciting. With this film, Roger Moore retired from the role of James Bond—having proven to the world that he could indeed walk proudly in Sean Connery's footsteps.

Q373. To what Beach Boys song does Bond snow surf in the opening sequence?

Q374. Who sings it in the film?

Questions

Q375. Who is the character played by Patrick Macnee?

Q376. What is the code name of Max Zorin's (Christopher Walken) operation to destroy silicon valley?

Q377. Who is the agent assigned to help Bond in San Francisco, only to be murdered by Zorin's men?

Q378. What later star had a small role in the film?

Q379. What is the suggestive name of actress Alison Doody's character?

Q380. Name the German doctor who is the mentor of Zorin.

Q381. Who composed the music for the film?

Q382. What group performs the smash hit title song?

Q383. Who plays Stacey Sutton?

Q384. What is Stacey's profession?

Q385. What cover story does Bond use to meet Stacey for the first time?

Q386. What alias does he use?

Q387. Where does Patrick Macnee's character meet his demise?

Q388. Zorin thinks Bond has drowned when the latter's car plummets into a lake. How does 007 survive underwater?

Q389. Where does the climactic fight between Bond and Zorin take place?

Q390. Who is Stacey's corrupt boss (who happens to be on Zorin's payroll)?

Q391. Why is Stacey's shotgun ineffective against the intruders Bond is shooting at?

Q392. Who is the beautiful KGB agent who Bond shares a hot tub with?

Q393. Actor Patrick Bauchau plays what vicious character?

Q394. What medal does General Gogol (Walter Gotell) want awarded to Bond?

Q395. What "fee" does Zorin demand from the manufacturers of microchips in return for destroying silicon valley?

Q396. What does Bond cook for Stacey in her kitchen?

Q397. Who is the French detective assassinated while dining with Bond in the Eiffel Tower?

Q398. What vehicle does Zorin use to escape the carnage at the mine he has destroyed?

Q399. What character's life is sacrificed by bringing the bomb back into the mine?

The Living Daylights

With Roger Moore retiring from Her Majesty's Secret Service, Cubby Broccoli once again engaged in a worldwide talent hunt for the next Bond actor. Many names had been tossed about in the press as "shoo-ins," but it was Shakespearean actor Timothy Dalton who emerged the dark horse winner. Dalton's debut as Bond in the 1987 film *The Living Daylights* was a true delight for hardcore 007 fans who thought they would never again see a serious entry in the series. Every bit as spectacular as the previous films,

Daylights also benefited from an excellent script by Richard Maibaum and Michael G. Wilson, and Dalton's intense, highly dramatic interpretation of Bond. The movie went on to become an international hit, and it appeared as though the Dalton era was about to begin.

Q400. In what city does Bond first see Kara?

Q401. Who plays Kara?

Q402. What is Kara's profession?

Q403. Who is the defecting Soviet officer whom Bond helps escape to the west?

Q404. A veteran of the Bond team makes a cameo appearance and is seen as a member of the audience at the opera in Vienna. Who is it?

Q405. Who makes a cameo appearance as the orchestra conductor in *Daylights's* finale?

Q406. Name the arms dealer who is behind the Soviet general's double cross.

Q407. Who is Bond's British Intelligence contact in Czechoslovakia and Vienna?

Q408. Who plays him?

Q409. Who plays Miss Moneypenny in this film?

Q410. Where does "M" instruct Bond to pick up a package enroute to the debriefing of Koskov?

Q411. Who is the Afghan rebel leader who joins forces with Bond?

Q412. What does "Q" call the lethal portable stereo system he has developed for the Americans?

Timothy Dalton drops in to play Bond in *The Living Daylights*

Q413. Who sings the film's title song?

Q414. Moneypenny invites Bond over to listen to her collection of what singer's records?

Questions

Q415. What is the name of the song heard over the end credits?

Q416. Who sings it?

Q417. What car does "Q" provide to Bond this time around?

Q418. Who plays General Pushkin?

Q419. At what European location does the double-0 training exercise in the pre-credits sequence take place?

Q420. What does the assassin Necros (Andreas Wisniewski) disguise himself as in order to kidnap Koskov from MI 5?

Q421. What does Kara call her Stradivarius cello?

Q422. What tune does Bond have to hum to activate the stun gas mechanism in his key ring device?

Q423. Which double-0 agent is murdered in the pre-credits sequence?

Q424. In what city does Whitaker reside?

Licence to Kill

Timothy Dalton's second (and last) film as James Bond remains one of the most controversial of the series. Anyone hoping the movies would continue to be dramatic certainly got their wish. *Licence* is the most realistic Bond film since *OHMSS,* and finds 007 having resigned from the Secret Service to embark on a highly personal mission of revenge. Although the film tested strongly in previews, general audiences and Bond fans complained that the film was *too* intense and Dalton's exceptional performance was criticized by many for being too sinister. The feeling was that *Licence* may have been a good thriller, but it didn't seem like a Bond movie—it was too dark and foreboding. Backed by a lackluster ad campaign and released in competition with other powerhouse films, it proved to be a box-office disappointment. At the same time, Cubby Broccoli's Eon Productions entered protracted legal problems with the (then) owners of MGM/UA, the company which had distribution rights to the series. It would be six years before another Bond movie would appear.

Q425. Where was principal photography shot for the film?

Q426. What is the name of Felix Leiter's (David Hedison) wife?

Q427. Who sings the title song?

Q428. Who composed the score?

Q429. What is the name of the character played by Wayne Newton?

Q430. The role of President Lopez is played by the son of a prominent supporting actor from *From Russia With Love*. Name him.

Q431. What song which plays over the end credits is sung by Patti LaBelle and would become a major hit years later with a rendition by Celine Dion?

Q432. The title *Licence to Kill* is unique among the Bond films as they pertain to the Ian Fleming source novels. Why?

Q433. Who is the captain of the ship which serves as a front for archvillain Franz Sanchez's (Robert Davi) operations?

Q434. What veteran actor portrays him?

Q435. Whom does Carey Lowell play?

Q436. What is the name of the bar from which Bond escapes in the Florida keys?

Q437. What gift does Leiter give Bond as a memento from his wedding?

Q438. What does the note attached to Leiter's shark-ravaged body read?

Q439. Who is Sanchez's financial mastermind?

Q440. Name the Hong Kong narcotics agent who captures and reprimands Bond for interfering with his operation?

Q441. At the end of the film, Bond's dilemma of being torn between Pam and Lupe Lamora (Talisa Soto) is resolved when the latter finds another date. With whom does Lupe link up?

Q442. What type of pet does Sanchez have perched on his shoulder in the pre-credits scene?

Q443. Name the Bond ally whose body is brought to "The Wavecrest" ship.

Q444. From what city does Sanchez run his drug empire?

Q445. Name the actor playing Sanchez's murderous henchman Dario.

Q446. When Bond arrives at his hotel, he is told at the desk that his "uncle" is awaiting him. Who does it turn out to be?

Q447. Who plays "M"?

Timothy Dalton and Carey Lowell in *Licence to Kill,* Dalton's second and last Bond epic.

Q448. What is the name of the corrupt drug enforcement agent who helps Sanchez escape from custody?

Q449. Who plays him?

GoldenEye

Frustrated by the delay in getting another Bond movie off the ground, and perhaps irritated by the lackluster reception given to *Licence To Kill,* Timothy Dalton shocked Eon Productions by resigning from the series just as the legal problems had been cleared and pre-production was to begin on the first 007 film in six years—*GoldenEye.* This time, there wasn't much suspense as to who would be the next Bond. Pierce Brosnan, an earlier favorite for the role, was signed amid a worldwide frenzy of press coverage. Brosnan nervously admitted that he did not know if there was still an audience for a Bond film, and took the entire responsibility for the future of the series on his shoulders. With the winter 1995 release of the movie, all doubts were quieted. *GoldenEye* received some of the best reviews of the series, and Brosnan was hailed as the best Bond since Connery. The movie would go on to gross well in excess of $300 million, making it the first 007 blockbuster since the 1960s. As of now, it appears as though a new era is at hand and Brosnan is the once and future Agent 007.

Q450. What is the double-0 number for Alec Trevelyan (Sean Bean)?

Q451. Name the Russian general who is working for Trevelyan.

Q452. What is the code name for Trevelyan's criminal alter ego?

Q453. What significance does the name GoldenEye have to the life of Ian Fleming?

Q454. Who is the CIA contact who works with Bond?

Q455. Who plays him?

Q456. In which previous Bond film did this actor appear, and in what role?

Q457. In addition to the Aston Martin DB5, Bond drives what new, high-profile car?

Q458. How many of the devices described by "Q" on this car does Bond employ during the film?

Q459. At MI 5, Bond and a fellow agent trade jokes about "M"—until "M" overhears them. Who is the slightly embarrassed agent (also a character in several of the Fleming novels)?

Q460. In the film, Bond is referred to as "a sexist, misogynist dinosaur." Who delivers this "compliment?"

Q461. Russian mafia godfather Valentin Zukovsky is portrayed by what popular British actor known for his portrayal of the TV detective "Cracker"?

Q462. Who sings the title song and what popular rock stars wrote it?

Q463. Who composed the musical score?

Q464. Who plays "M"?

Q465. Who is the woman from MI 5 sent to evaluate Bond, only to be seduced by him?

The Bond for the '90s and beyond—Pierce Brosnan in the smash hit *GoldenEye*

Q466. How does Xenia Onatopp (Famke Janssen) like her alcohol?

Q467. Who plays Natalya and what is her last name?

Q468. Who is assigned to interrogate Bond after he is captured by the Russians?

Q469. Who plays Moneypenny?

Q470. Who wrote the screenplay?

Q471. Where is Trevelyan's satellite station located?

Q472. What type of helicopter does Xenia steal from the French military?

Q473. In what city does Bond pursue Ourumov in a tank?

Q474. *GoldenEye* is dedicated to a veteran member of the Bond team who passed away shortly after principal photography was completed. Who was this master technician?

Top Secret Multiple Choice Quiz

Q475. In what year did Ian Fleming die?

    A. 1962
    B. 1963
    C. 1964
    D. 1965

Q476. In which novel does Bond attempt to assassinate "M"?

    A. *Live and Let Die*
    B. *The Man With the Golden Gun*

C. *You Only Live Twice*
D. *Diamonds Are Forever*

Q477. In the early 1980s, novelist John Gardner began writing new adventure novels starring James Bond. Which was the first Gardner novel?

A. *For Special Services*
B. *Icebreaker*
C. *Licence Renewed*
D. *Brokenclaw*

Q478. Who played James Bond in the 1954 CBS TV broadcast of *Casino Royale*?

A. Hoagy Charmichael
B. Stanley Baker
C. Barry Nelson
D. Richard Johnson

Q479. Ian Fleming "borrowed" the name James Bond from the real-life author of what book?

A. *My Life in the O.S.S.*
B. *An Adventurer's Guide to Jamaica*
C. *The Odessa File*
D. *Birds of the West Indies*

Q480. Ian Fleming's World War II experiences were dramatized in a TV movie starring which one of the following actors?

A. Patrick Macnee
B. Jason Connery
C. Neil Connery
D. David McCallum

Ian Fleming, the prolific writer whose fertile imagination gave birth to Agent 007

Q481. In the movie *Dr. No,* the title villain meets his death when he slides into a radioactive pool. How did he die in the novel?

    A. He was accidentally incinerated by the dragon tank.
    B. He slipped on a banana peel provided to Bond by "Q" Branch.
    C. He was buried in bird guano.
    D. He died of tetanus when his metal hands rusted.

Q482. In the novel *From Russia With Love,* Bond kills Red Grant with a knife concealed in which book?

   A. *Gone With the Wind*
   B. *War and Peace*
   C. *The Holy Bible*
   D. *The Kama Sutra*

Q483. In 1967, Sean Connery's brother Neil appeared in which low-budget ripoff of the 007 films that has since become a camp classic?

   A. *For Your Thighs Only*
   B. *Thunderballs*
   C. *Operation Kid Brother*
   D. *James Bond Jr.*

Q484. Danjaq, the company founded by Cubby Broccoli and Harry Saltzman, had its name derived from:

   A. A Swiss holding company they purchased
   B. The names of their wives
   C. The names of their children
   D. A cousin of Ian Fleming's

Q485. Which famous children's novel did Ian Fleming author?

   A. *Mary Poppins*
   B. *The Little Engine That Could*
   C. *Those Magnificent Men in Their Flying Machines*
   D. *Chitty Chitty Bang Bang*

Q486. Which nonfictional book represented Ian Fleming's experiences with exotic locations?

   A. *Thrilling Cities*
   B. *Erotic Locales of the Orient*
   C. *A Spy's Guide to Europe and the Orient*
   D. *Wine, Women and Song on $10 a Day*

Q487. Which popular TV series did Fleming play a minor role in developing?
- A. *I Spy*
- B. *The Man From U.N.C.L.E.*
- C. *The Saint*
- D. *The Flying Nun*

Q488. *Dr. No* was not originally supposed to be the first Bond film. Which Fleming novel was being developed initially to introduce 007 to movie fans?
- A. *Goldfinger*
- B. *From Russia With Love*
- C. *Thunderball*
- D. *Live and Let Die*

Q489. In the mid-1970s Sean Connery cowrote the screenplay for a James Bond film which never came to fruition. What was it titled?
- A. *Captain Jamaica*
- B. *Warhead*
- C. *James Bond, Secret Agent*
- D. *Spy Hard*

Q490. What is the real first name of the villain Red Grant in the Fleming novel?
- A. Donald
- B. Donovan
- C. Boris
- D. Murray

Q491. In the novel *The Man With the Golden Gun*, what is Scaramanga's nickname?
- A. Pistols
- B. Sureshot
- C. Deadeye
- D. Bullseye

Questions

Q492. The Bond phenomenon took off after President John F. Kennedy listed a 007 novel among his ten favorite books of all time. Which Bond thriller was it?

    A. *Goldfinger*
    B. *Thunderball*
    C. *Dr. No*
    D. *From Russia With Love*

Q493. Sean Connery first came to the attention of Cubby Broccoli and his wife Dana when they saw him in which movie?

    A. *The Longest Day*
    B. *Another Time, Another Place*
    C. *The Frightened City*
    D. *Darby O'Gill and the Little People*

Q494. Prior to *On Her Majesty's Secret Service*, the only acting experience George Lazenby had ever had was in what?

    A. Regional theater productions
    B. A candy commercial
    C. Australian news shows as a sports commentator
    D. College stage shows

Q495. George Lazenby had a cameo role as a thinly-veiled Bond character in which TV movie?

    A. *The Return of Maxwell Smart*
    B. *The Return of the Man From U.N.C.L.E.*
    C. *I Spy Returns*
    D. *The Wild, Wild West Revisited*

Q496. Approached for the role of Bond in 1970, Timothy Dalton turned down the producers because:

    A. They could not meet his salary demands.
    B. He and Vanessa Redgrave were committed to doing a series of plays in London's West End.
    C. He was too intimidated to take over from Sean Connery.
    D. He was contracted to do a remake of *Wuthering Heights*.

Q497. How many Oscar winners have appeared in James Bond films?

    A. One
    B. Two
    C. Three
    D. Four

Q498. In how many films does Bond *not* wear a tuxedo?

    A. One
    B. Two
    C. Three
    D. Four

Q499. Prior to *Goldfinger*, Sean Connery and Gert Frobe appeared in what other film together?

    A. *The Frightened City*
    B. *The Longest Day*
    C. *Operation Snafu*
    D. *Tarzan's Greatest Adventure*

Q500. Prior to the first Bond film, Terence Young directed Sean Connery in what movie?

    A. *Time Lock*
    B. *No Road Back*
    C. *Action of the Tiger*
    D. *Hell Drivers*

Q501. Pierce Brosnan had actually been signed years ago to play James Bond. However, a conflict with his contract with *Remington Steele* on TV prevented him from taking the role. What Bond film was he to have appeared in?

  A. *A View to a Kill*
  B. *The Living Daylights*
  C. *Licence to Kill*
  D. *Never Say Never Again*

James Bond Trivia Answers

Dr. No—Answers

A1. Professor Dent, Dr. No's right-hand man

A2. Anthony Dawson

A3. She placed a black widow spider in his bed.

A4. The Tongs

A5. Major Boothroyd

A6. Peter Burton, in his one-shot appearance in the role

A7. *Live and Let Die.* "Q" was written out of the script at the last minute, much to the dismay of the fans—and Desmond Llewelyn.

A8. John Strangways, the Jamaican-based representative of MI 5.

A9. Miss Trueblood

A10. Zena Marshall

A11. *From Russia With Love,* the follow-up. The character was supposed to recur in all future Bond films, but when Terence Young, the director of the first two 007 adventures, left the series temporarily, the character vanished and has not been seen since.

A12. "Underneath the Mango Tree"

A13. Crab Key, Jamaica

A14. Stunt coordinator Bob Simmons filled in for Connery in the first three Bond films. Ultimately, the actual actor who played Bond would be seen in the gun-barrel of all future films. Simmons was a stuntman extraordinaire who would have a long association with the series, doubling for both heroes and villains. He would also double for Sean Connery in several of his non-Bond films, including the 1968 Western *Shalako*.

A15. Fleming's good friend and fellow resident on Jamaica, Nöel Coward

A16. Special Executor for Counterintelligence, Terrorism, Revenge, and Extortion

A17. Puss-Feller

A18. Maurice Binder, who would go on to create the majority of the main titles in the series until his death in 1992. He was a true pioneer in his field and his contributions to the Bond films, as well as other major motion pictures, cannot be overstated.

A19. Mr. Jones. The would-be "hit man" takes cyanide rather than suffer retribution from Dr. No himself.

A20. Bond reluctantly must relinquish his trusty Baretta. He argues with "M" to allow him to keep it, but the latter sides with Boothroyd, who calls it appropriate only for a ladies handbag. Bond is assured that his new Walther has "a delivery like a brick through a plate glass window."

Answers

A21. Metallic hands

A22. Peter Hunt. A long time veteran of the series, he would later go on to direct such non-Bond epics as *Gold* and *Shout at the Devil,* both of which starred Roger Moore.

A23. Felix Leiter

A24. Jack Lord, later to play McGarrett on TV's *Hawaii Five-O*

A25. Monty Norman is officially credited, although there has long been speculation among Bond fans that John Barry was the true originator of the theme, but had to give Norman credit for contractual reasons.

From Russia With Love—Answers

A26. Walter Gotell

A27. Jan Williams

A28. At Pinewood Studios, England, the longtime home of the Bond films and nearly every other major British-based movie for decades. The Bond team ultimately had to move from Pinewood in the nineties for the shooting of *GoldenEye* when the studio proved unavailable due to the presence of the Sean Connery film *First Knight*. So, ironically it was the man who originated 007 on-screen who was responsible for dispossessing his fictional alter ego! (The Bond filmmakers would convert an abandoned Rolls Royce factory outside London to the largest film studio in Europe for *GoldenEye*.)

A29. Martine Beswick and Aliza Gur

A30. One minute, 52 seconds

A31. Siamese fighting fish, who are occasionally fed to Blofeld's pet Siamese cat

A32. Number 3

A33. Number 5

A34. Mr. McAdams of Canada

A35. Twenty

A36. Rug merchant, located in a busy bazaar

A37. Circus strongman who could bend steel bars with his teeth

A38. He tells the front desk that the bed is too small. The bug was intended to be discovered, however, and Bond is "conveniently" moved to the bridal suite where he meets Tania—the bait for the S.P.E.C.T.R.E. trap.

A39. Krilencu (Fred Haggerty), who leads the assault on the gypsy camp in an attempt to kill Bey

A40. *Call Me Bwana*, the Bob Hope-Anita Ekberg comedy which is featured as the billboard on the side of Krilencu's hideout

A41. Mr. and Mrs. David Somerset

A42. Commissar Benz (Peter Bayliss), a KGB operative

A43. Captain Nash, whose identity Grant assumes to gain Bond's confidence. The role was played by the film's production manager, Bill Hill.

A44. Grilled sole and red wine

A45. Twelve seconds, prompting Blofeld to complain about the need for a faster working venom

A46. Venice

A47. Martine Beswick. Her name appears as "Martin." (Anyone who views her in her gypsy girl outfit, however, will be more than convinced of her true gender!)

A48. Leila

A49. In her interrogation by Rosa Klebb, she admits to having had three. Klebb, who places her hand on Tatiana's knee, clearly has intentions of becoming number four!

A50. Matt Munro sings it; Lionel Bart (who did the musical *Oliver!*) wrote it.

Goldfinger—Answers

A51. BMT 216A

A52. England, Switzerland, and France

A53. Operation Grand Slam

A54. Mr. Solo, the Mafia hood whose disagreement with Goldfinger leads to his "pressing appointment" in the car crusher. During production, it was reported that the cast and crew considered the destruction of a new Lincoln Continental to be a virtually sacreligious act!

A55. Tania Mallet

A56. A Rolls Royce

A57. Alf Joint, a well-known stuntman in England. He got the job on short notice when the actor originally selected for the part was arrested the night before filming on charges of being a cat burglar!

A58. A heater

A59. In Miami Beach, at the Fountainbleu Hotel, to be precise. The exteriors were shot on location, but all the footage of Bond and Goldfinger was filmed at Pinewood Studios in England. Neither Sean Connery nor Gert Frobe ever set foot in Miami.

A60. Auric. The name reminds James Bond of "a French nail polish."

A61. "I must be dreaming."

A62. Slazenger #1

A63. Delta 9. When Bond appeals to Goldfinger's "humanitarianism" by reminding him that his nerve gas will kill thousands of innocent people, Goldfinger nonchalantly reminds him that "American motorists kill that many every two years!"

A64. 007 seconds. Originally, the script called for the bomb to stop at "003" seconds. Producer Harry Saltzman came up with the idea for 007 seconds after the scene had been shot. An insert of the counter at "007" was added, but as Connery had already completed filming, the movie still has him referring to "three more ticks."

A65. Mr. Ling

A66. Kato, Inspector Clouseau's long-suffering servant from the *Pink Panther* films.

Answers

A67. A military ambulance

A68. Mint Julip

A69. Kentucky, although Bond fans may be surprised to learn that all of this footage was shot on the backlot at Pinewood Studios

A70. Michael Mellinger

A71. Cec Linder

A72. Norman Wanstall won for Best Achievement in Sound.

A73. Revolving license plates

A74. There is a brief shot of Bond running from the helicopter in *From Russia With Love*. This particular shot does not actually appear in that film; the footage used in *Goldfinger* must have been an outtake.

Thunderball—Answers

A75. Rose Alba plays the woman in the beginning of the scene. However, once Bond socks her, stuntman Bob Simmons takes over the role.

A76. Volpe

A77. A cigar and ice cubes. As for how he intends to use both of these, it is better that screenwriters Richard Maibaum and John Hopkins left this to our imaginations!

A78. Professor Kutze, the Polish physicist who has second thoughts about his alliance with the evil Largo

A79. John Stears won for Special Visual Effects

A80. Philip Locke

A81. Café Martinique, a lush dining establishment in Nassau which still operates

A82. Jacques Boitier

A83. Rik Van Nutter. He was the husband of actress Anita Ekberg, who costarred in *Call Me Bwana* for Broccoli and Saltzman. The couple was dining with the Broccolis one evening when he was offered the role of Leiter. While his remains one of the more popular interpretations of the role, for reasons unknown the producers did not follow through on their original plans to use him in future Bond films.

A84. Palmyra. Sean Connery now maintains a residence on Paradise Island on the grounds where some of the location work was shot.

A85. Paris. The organization masquerades as an agency which provides social services for refugees.

A86. An octopus

A87. Count Lippe (Guy Doleman), who has been sentenced to death for his failure to terminate 007

A88. Shrublands. The building is now owned by the British Aluminium Company, located near Pinewood Studios. Although abandoned, it is maintained in excellent condition, and the company patiently tolerates the numbers of 007 fans who visit it every year.

A89. A common broom, but it suffices in making Lippe "burn up"

A90. Mollie Peters

Answers

A91. Miami Beach

A92. Four minutes—although Bond inexplicably uses it for a period of time far in excess of four minutes during the climactic battle sequence

A93. Major Derval, Domino's brother

A94. A Vulcan Bomber complete with two live atomic bombs

A95. The Kiss-Kiss Club. It was originally called the "Jump Jump Club," but the name was changed when plans were made for the title song to the film to be "Mr. Kiss Kiss Bang Bang." Dionne Warwick recorded the tune, and it was felt the club would tie in to the song. At the last minute, however, it was decided to have the song entitled "Thunderball." The Warwick tune is only heard in John Barry's instrumental version.

A96. Felix Leiter and the Coast Guard

A97. "I think he got the point."

A98. Paula

A99. Tom Jones

Casino Royale—Answers

A100. Woody Allen

A101. Ursula Andress, who was the first "Bond girl" in *Dr. No*

A102. Herb Alpert and the Tijuana Brass

A103. "The Look of Love," as sung by Dusty Springfield. Later, Sergio Mendes and Brasil '66 had a hit single with their rendition of it.

A104. Peter O'Toole, who identifies himself as Richard Burton

A105. John Huston, Val Guest, Robert Parrish, Ken Hughes, and Joseph McGrath

A106. Terence Cooper

A107. Ransome

A108. "A hair loom"

A109. Burt Kwouk (Mr. Ling in *Goldfinger*) and Vladek Sheybal (Kronsteen in *From Russia With Love*)

A110. Evelyn Tremble

A111. Miss Goodthighs. Note that the then-unknown actress is billed as "Jackie Bisset."

A112. Barbara Bouchet

A113. Peter Lorre

A114. In the beginning sequence, the heads of the various intelligence agencies drive through Bond's estate and encounter a pride of lions. Barry's theme from *Born Free* is heard—at least a few bars of it.

A115. A black rose

A116. Dr. Noah

A117. George Raft, who, along with several other actors such as Jean Paul Belmondo, received prominent billing even though their on-screen appearances lasted only seconds

Answers

A118. Mata Hari

A119. SMERSH

A120. To kill all men over four feet six and make all women beautiful

A121. Burt Bacharach

A122. John Huston

A123. He becomes so intimidated, he loses the ability to speak.

A124. Stuttering

You Only Live Twice—Answers

A125. Roald Dahl. Fleming's source novel was a moody, dark adventure in which Bond goes to Japan to infiltrate Blofeld's ancient castle, including a notorious "Garden of Death" designed to discourage trespassers. Although he defeats Blofeld, Bond is injured and suffers from total amnesia. Unable to report back to MI 5, "M" assumes that his most valued agent is dead. Dahl's screenplay for the film became the first instance of discarding virtually every aspect of a source novel and replacing it with an original storyline. Aside from the geographical settings and the presence of several characters from the book, the film version of *You Only Live Twice* was a hi-tech, big-budget affair replete with space capsules and the threat of nuclear war.

A126. Akiko Wakabayashi

A127. Her name is never mentioned once.

A128. Mr. Henderson, a British agent who is killed as he is about to reveal a key plot point to Bond

A129. Donald Pleasance was a last-minute choice for the part, following the departure of Jan Werlich, who became ill just before filming began.

A130. Mie Hama. She and Akiko Wakabayashi were slated to play each other's role when the film initially went into production. At the last minute the actresses' parts were switched.

A131. Tiger Tanaka (played by Tetsuro Tamba)

A132. "I love you."

A133. *Ning Po*. The vessel serves as the storage area for tanks of liquid nitrogen which Blofeld is amassing to use as rocket fuel.

A134. Mr. Osato (played by Teru Shimada)

A135. Helga Brandt (Karin Dor), the seductive temptress who advises Bond about the necessity of maintaining a "healthy chest"

A136. She falls victim to Blofeld's pool of piranha fish.

A137. Aboard the submarine named *M 1*

A138. Inside a dormant volcano

A139. Hans

A140. Ken Adam. Here he created the ultimate set for a Bond film—the S.P.E.C.T.R.E. volcano. Miniatures were not used and Adam built a full-scale set for a then-whopping $1 million. The gigantic masterpiece of production design was touted by one critic as being incredible enough to be a World's Fair attraction. For whatever reason, Adam's work did not receive an Oscar nomination.

A141. Hong Kong

A142. Ling

A143. He poses as a poor fisherman—assuming the island has plenty of six-foot-three fishermen with Scottish accents!

A144. Poisonous gas

A145. Three

A146. The incredible auto-gyro brought to Japan by "Q." Bond uses the mini-helicopter to investigate the location of the stolen space ships as he flies over Japan. In the process, he is attacked by a fleet of S.P.E.C.T.R.E. choppers and must utilize the high-powered arsenal with which "Q" has equipped Little Nellie (i.e., machine guns, rockets, and heat-seeking missiles). The aircraft was designed by Ken Wallis, who also flew the plane in the film and continues to showcase Little Nellie in air shows. He has built an exact replica of the plane which is on display at Planet Hollywood in London.

A147. None. Bond is never seen driving. Aki drives the Toyota in which Bond rides several times in the film.

A148. He says, "She has the face of a pig!" Of course, Bond learns he is being set up for a joke after he sees that his "bride" will be the gorgeous Kissy Suzuki.

A149. Nancy Sinatra

On Her Majesty's Secret Service—Answers

A150. Piz Gloria

A151. Honey Rider's knife from *Dr. No*; the rebreather device from *Thunderball;* and Red Grant's wristwatch from *From Russia With Love*.

A152. Diana Rigg (Tracy) starred in *The Avengers* and Joanna Lumley (English girl) starred in "The New Avengers"

A153. Irma Bundt (played by Ilse Steppat)

A154. Sir Hilary Bray, from the College of Arms

A155. "The World Is Not Enough"

A156. Marc Ange Draco (played by Gabriele Ferzetti), the charismatic and powerful organized crime chieftain

A157. The lack of earlobes

A158. A ruler and an eraser

A159. One million pounds, to which Bond casually replies, "I don't need a million pounds." Talk about a confirmed bachelor!

A160. His hat

A161. Portugal

A162. Collecting butterflies

A163. Campbell (played by Bernard Horsfall)

A164. Peter Hunt

A165. A janitor is whistling a few bars from "Goldfinger."

A166. She secretly uses lipstick to write it on his leg.

Answers

A167. A portrait of Queen Elizabeth

A168. Radioactive lint. In the pre-credits scene Bond tries unsuccessfully to interest "M" in this miraculous device.

A169. A boar's head

A170. Irma Bundt

A171. "We Have All the Time in the World"

A172. Louis Armstrong

A173. Aston Martin DB5

A174. Bond, cradling his deceased wife in his arms, tells a policeman, "We have all the time in the world."

Diamonds Are Forever—Answers

A175. He played Mr. Henderson in *You Only Live Twice*.

A176. Peter Franks

A177. Actor/stuntman Joe Robinson

A178. As a customs official. Ironically, this was the first film in which Lois Maxwell was contractually allowed to keep her wardrobe after shooting. She was dismayed to find the clothes were useless, unless she wanted to join British Customs!

A179. Marc Lawrence

A180. Actor/country singer/ sausage magnate Jimmy Dean. The role of Whyte was based on Howard Hughes, with whom Cubby Broccoli had been friendly. The plot scheme was inspired by a dream which Cubby had in which Bond is captured by a man pretending to be Hughes.

A181. Bruce Glover (father of brat pack actor Crispin Glover) is Mr. Wint and Putter Smith is the inimitable Mr. Kidd. Smith, a jazz musician who had never acted before, was chosen for the role because of his rather unorothdox physical appearance.

A182. A Mustang Mach 1

A183. Bruce Cabot, veteran actor and long ago star of *King Kong*. The role of Saxby, the corrupt pit boss in league with Blofeld would be Cabot's last. Incidentally, note the nameplate on his desk during one sequence. It reads "Albert R. Saxby"—an "in joke" directed at Albert R. Broccoli.

A184. Klaus Hergersheimer, the hapless man in charge of checking the dependency of radiation shields

A185. Mrs. Whistler. Her Amsterdam schoolhouse serves as a cover for the diamond smuggling operation.

A186. Shirley Bassey, her second association with the Bond series, previously having sung the chart-topping title song to *Goldfinger*

A187. The Whyte House. In actuality it was the Las Vegas Hilton, then owned by Howard Hughes. Hughes gave the filmmakers permission to shoot there in exchange for a 16mm print of the movie.

A188. The female acrobats assigned to guard Willard Whyte, played by Trina Parks and Donna Garrett

A189. He places them in the rectum of smuggler Peter Franks, whom Bond pretends is his dearly departed brother. When Felix Leiter (Norman Burton) asks where the diamonds are hidden on the body, 007 replies, "Alimentary, my dear Felix."

Answers

A190. Shady Tree

A191. Leonard Barr, a popular stand-up comedian who also happened to be Dean Martin's uncle

A192. He lingers over her cleavage and notes, "But of course you are."

A193. Marie. Bond rips off her bikini top, tangles it around her neck, and threatens to strangle her after offering to help her get something off her chest.

A194. Sammy Davis Jr., who was slated for a cameo in the film, and in fact shot the sequence. However, director Guy Hamilton felt it was extraneous and the scene ended up on the cutting room floor.

A195. The Bath-O-Sub, a mini-submarine which is lowered by crane into the water. Bond commandeers the crane and gives Blofeld a memorable ride!

A196. Off the coast of Baja, California

A197. Bert Saxby's. Bond is able to convince Blofeld he is Saxby by utilizing a device from "Q" which allows one to imitate any other person's voice.

A197. Sir Donald Munger, played by the late Laurence Naismith

A199. Dr. Tynan

Live and Let Die—Answers

A200. Mr. Big

A201. San Monique—one of the few fictitious locations Bond has visited

A202. Whisper (played by Earl Jolly Brown)

A203. He cuts the wires with a pair of scissors.

A204. Best song. Paul and Linda McCartney wrote and performed the tune, but it lost at Oscar time to "The Way We Were."

A205. George Martin, the producer of most of the Beatles' albums.

A206. She allows Bond to take away her virginity.

A207. Billy Bob, who attempts to stop Bond by utilizing the fastest speedboat on the bayou. However, he is rendered unconscious and the boat is stolen by one of Kananga's thugs.

A208. Distinctive Geoffrey Holder, the Tony-winning choreographer of many Broadway hits.

A209. Baines, who is murdered when Samedi places a poisonous snake near his face

A210. A magnetic watch. Bond tries using it to pull a rowboat to him but is thwarted when he finds the boat is tied to the dock. He ultimately must run across the backs of the gators to escape certain death.

A211. Mrs. Bell

A212. Filet of Soul, which has two locations—Harlem and New Orleans

A213. He asks her to tell him the serial number on the back of Bond's watch

A214. Gloria Hendry. The film marked the first Bond movie to feature 007 in an inter-racial romance.

Answers

A215. Bond's coffee maker, which is elaborate enough to rival anything created by "Q"

A216. Quarrel Jr., son of Quarrel, Bond's heroic helper from *Dr. No*

A217. *Dr. No*. Here Bond seduces—or rather, is seduced—by Sylvia Trench, whom he finds playing golf attired only in a dress shirt, sans pants.

A218. A hat on the bed

A219. Jamming a pencil behind its eye and reaching into its mouth and pulling out its teeth

A220. Old Albert—undoubtedly another good-natured joke at Albert Broccoli's expense

A221. *The Man With the Golden Gun,* the next Bond film. Pepper's over-the-top humor quickly wore thin, however, and the lawman was retired from the series.

A222. Strutter, who compliments Bond on his "clever disguise" on being the only white face in Harlem

A223. Miss Caruso. She and Bond are caught in coitus interuptus when "M" decides to drop in at 007's apartment. It's up to Moneypenny to bail Bond out by hiding Miss Caruso.

A224. Tom Mankiewicz, who introduced much of the lighthearted humor that would characterize the Roger Moore Bonds.

The Man With the Golden Gun—Answers

A225. Chew Me

A226. He has sex with his mistress.

A227. She later plays the title role in *Octopussy* and is one of the few actresses to appear in more than one Bond film.

A228. Clifton James as Sheriff Pepper

A229. "The Bottoms Up Club"

A230. Gibson

A231. Veteran character actor Richard Loo

A232. *Queen Elizabeth I*

A233. Lulu

A234. Actor Marc Lawrence played the gangster who manhandled Plenty O'Toole in *Diamonds Are Forever.*

A235. American Motors Hornet

A236. Nick Nack

A237. Herve Villechaize, later to find fame on *Fantasy Island*

A238. Mary Goodnight, Bond's airheaded colleague from British Secret Service

A239. Lt. Hip, played by Soon-Taik Oh

A240. One million dollars—and he only requires one shot

A241. A third nipple

A242. An old-time fun house, where the props fire lethal weapons at unsuspecting intruders

Answers

A243. They "borrow" the recently-deceased Scaramanga's Chinese junk.

A244. He was Agent 002.

A245. In a belly dancer's navel. She is using it as a good luck charm.

A246. Lt. Hip and his two nieces—who are coincidentally experts at Kung Fu

A247. December 1974

A248. The *Battle of Britain*

A249. John Barry

The Spy Who Loved Me—Answers

A250. Best Song ("Nobody Does It Better"); Best Musical Score, and Best Art Direction.

A251. Shane Rimmer

A252. Webbed fingers

A253. Sandor

A254. Fekkesh

A255. Agent Triple X

A256. Sergei Barsov. Bond kills him during a ski chase. Upon learning this, Anya swears to avenge his death.

A257. Naomi

A258. Caroline Munro, the vivacious "scream queen" primarily known for her sexy roles in horror films

A259. Rick Sylvester. The stunt was inspired by a print ad featuring Sylvester skiing off a mountain. Cubby Broccoli was so intrigued by the premise that he hired Sylvester to perform the impressive stunt as the opening for the Bond film. The risky venture is still regarded as one of the screen's classic action setpieces.

A260. Geoffrey Keene

A261. Commander. However, this aspect of Bond's career is never stressed in the films. He appears in uniform only in *You Only Live Twice* and *The Spy Who Loved Me*.

A262. *The Liparus*. It is via this enormous vessel that Stromberg manages to steal U.S. and Soviet nuclear subs.

A263. Atlantis

A264. Lotus Esprit. Like the Aston Martin DB5 before it, the Lotus featured an amazing array of gadgets and weapons. Its most sensational "option" was the ability to transform into a fully functional submarine vehicle.

A265. PPW 306R

A266. By teletype which comes through Bond's wristwatch

A267. He uses a gadget which shoots a stream of cement onto the other vehicle's windshield.

A268. Max Kalba

A269. Admiral Hargreaves

A270. "Just keeping the British end up, sir!"

A271. Marvin Hamlisch

A272. Carly Simon

A273. *For Your Eyes Only* was announced as the next Bond epic. However, due to the success of *Star Wars,* the producers opted to capitalize on the space theme and made *Moonraker* the follow-up 007 epic.

Moonraker—Answers

A274. Michael Lonsdale

A275. Chang (Toshiro Suga). He takes to heart Drax's command to "Look after Mr. Bond. See that some harm comes to him."

A276. Venice

A277. Lois Chiles

A278. Not NASA, but Vasser

A279. Best Visual Effects. It lost to *Star Trek—The Motion Picture.*

A280. Shirley Bassey, her third and last Bond song to date

A281. Over the Yukon. Drax manages to hijack the shuttle despite the fact it is attached to a carrier plane.

A282. Apollo Airways

A283. Frederick Gray, played by Geoffrey Keen

A284. California. However, the exteriors of Drax's mansion were filmed in France, where much of *Moonraker* was shot, a striking departure from the filmmakers' customary use of Pinewood Studios.

A285. Cavendish (You were expecting maybe "Murray"?)

A286. Countess Lubinsky and Lady Victoria Devan

A287. Afternoon tea

A288. Twenty. Bond is trapped in the centrifuge when Chang takes over the controls and pushes the speed to the limit. Fortunately, Bond has a wristwatch gun which shoots a dart. At death's door, he manages to utilize the device to destroy the control panel in the centrifuge, thereby foiling Drax's plan to have 007's death appear to be an accident.

A289. Corinne Clery played this film's sacrificial lamb who is killed by Drax because she helps Bond. Her death is a particularly hideous one—she fails to outrun Drax's ravenous Dobermans. Like all Bond film sadism, however, more gore is implied than actually shown.

A290. Dolly, although it is never mentioned in the film

A291. "To us!" Jaws exclaims during a romantic interlude with Dolly on the destroyed space station from which Drax once planned to rule the universe. Prior to this, Jaws had converted to the side of law and order and assisted Bond in defeating Drax. He is now reunited with his lover, a buxom, pigtailed, but equally silent German lass. Not exactly a scene taken directly from Fleming's source novel!

A292. Venini Glass

A293. The notes from *Close Encounters of the Third Kind* symbolize the sound heard when Bond uses a secret code to enter a laboratory.

A294. Composer Elmer Bernstein's "The Magnificent Seven"

Answers

A295. Bollinger, 1969. Bollinger has long had ties to the James Bond films, and has been represented in most recent 007 epics, including *GoldenEye*. It is unofficially marketed as "The Champagne of James Bond."

A296. Emily Bolton

A297. Inside a monastery. Here the "monks" indulge in training programs using the exotic "Q" weaponry. Bond visits the site and finds that not only is "Q" present, but so are "M" and Moneypenny.

A298. In a perfume atomizer

For Your Eyes Only—Answers

A299. Although it is insinuated that it is Blofeld, the villain's name is never mentioned.

A300. The title theme was nominated for Best Song. Although it lost to "Arthur's Theme," it was presented in a gigantic stage spectacular during the Academy Award ceremonies, complete with an actor doubling for Bond, and veteran bad guys Richard Kiel and Harold Sakata taking part in the mayhem.

A301. Bill Conti, best known for his memorable theme from *Rocky*

A302. Sheena Easton. Her sexiness so impressed main titles designer Maurice Binder that he made her the first singer to actually appear in the main credits sequence.

A303. Bibbi Doll

A304. Topol, the actor best known for his many years of playing Tevye in *Fiddler on the Roof* on stage and screen

A305. Hector Gonzalez

A306. Editor John Glen, who would go on to direct four more Bond epics

A307. Bill Tanner, the chief of staff, played by James Villiers. Bernard Lee was preparing to return as "M," but died shortly before production began.

A308. Cassandra Harris. She would become Mrs. Pierce Brosnan. Sadly, she would die from cancer before seeing her husband get the role of Bond he sought for so long.

A309. Aris

A310. Julian Glover

A311. Locque (played by Michael Gothard). In fact, Roger Moore objected to the scene on the basis that the killing was too cold-blooded for *his* James Bond. The director argued that the situation called for harsh measures because Bond was avenging the death of his friend. Ultimately, Moore relented, and the scene turned out to be one of his best moments as 007.

A312. Margaret Thatcher. She is played by Janet Brown, who made a career of her uncanny impersonation of the (then) prime minister.

A313. Max

A314. At his late wife Tracy's grave site. This is one of the only references linking Roger Moore's films to the previous Bonds. Tracy, of course, was the ill-fated

Mrs. Bond seen in George Lazenby's film *On Her Majesty's Secret Service*.

A315. The *St. Georges*

A316. The ATAC, a decoding device which the British and Soviets are in a desperate separate race to recover

A317. Ferrara (John Moreno), the film's obligatory sacrificial lamb who is murdered by Locque

A318. "Risico"

A319. *Live and Let Die*. In that novel, Bond and Solitaire are keelhauled in much the same manner as Bond and Melina are. To add some spice, however, Fleming insured they were also naked in the book.

A320. "The Dove"

A321. A monastery in Greece, high atop a virtually inaccessible mountain. In reality, local monks objected to the filming and tried to disrupt sequences by hanging large banners in the vicinity of the shooting location.

A322. Jill Bennett

Octopussy—Answers

A323. Vijay Amritraj

A324. "All Time High"

A325. Rita Coolidge

A326. Orlov

A327. Penelope Smallbone. Played by Michaela Clavell, the daughter of famed novelist James Clavell, the character was obviously introduced in anticipation of replacing Moneypenny with a younger character when Roger Moore left the series. (*Octopussy* was supposed to be his last Bond film.) The casting was news to Lois Maxwell, who had not been aware of it until filming began. The situation was uncomfortable, as she knew that the Smallbone character was designed to put Moneypenny out to pasture. In a Freudian slip, Lois referred to the character as Penelope Smallbush, prompting the crew to crack up and Roger to joke, "We know where *your* mind has been, Miss Moneypenny!" Lois got the last laugh, however, when Roger signed for yet another Bond film and the services of Moneypenny were retained once again.

A328. Corkey Fornof, the designer of the remarkable craft, doubled for Roger Moore and flew the plane in the exciting opening sequence.

A329. Kamal Khan

A330. "The Property of a Lady." The title is mentioned by the auctioneer when he describes the egg.

A331. Agent 009

A332. The Monsoon Palace

A333. A large barge complete with female rowers—in halter tops, natch!

A334. Magda

A335. 007 snaps an antenna wire in his face.

Answers

A336. Vijay, disguised as a snake charmer, is heard playing a few bars of the Bond theme.

A337. A yo-yo with a built-in razor blade

A338. Colonel Toro (played by Ken Norris)

A339. "Operation Trove"

A340. Double sixes

A341. Stuffed sheep's head, with particular emphasis on the eyeballs

A342. An alligator, courtesy of "Q Branch"

A343. An octopus

A344. Jim Fanning (played by Douglas Wilmer)

A345. The Imperial State Coach of the Czar of Russia

A346. A fountain pen containing sulfuric acid which Bond uses to burn through steel bars

A347. David and Anthony Meyer

Never Say Never Again—Answers

A348. Edward Fox as the youngest, but unfriendliest "M" to date

A349. Pamela Salem, who also appeared with Connery in *The Great Train Robbery*

A350. Fatima Blush, femme fatale and S.P.E.C.T.R.E. assassin supreme. Carrera's entertaining performance earned her a Golden Globe nomination.

A351. Behind a bank vault

A352. "The Tears of Allah," based on a tale of a woman whose lover died, and who cried so much that her tears formed a well. "The Tears of Allah" also happens to be a clever joke designed by Largo, as unbeknownst to Domino, he has located his secret headquarters for a nuclear strike underground in an area accessible by a remote well.

A353. Maximillian, although in the source novel and in the film *Thunderball* it is Emilio

A354. Fatima Blush

A355. Capt. Jack Petachi (Gavan O'Herlihy), a NATO pilot Fatima has seduced, blackmailed, and addicted to drugs as part of forcing him to work for S.P.E.C.T.R.E.

A356. A urine specimen, which blinds Lippe and causes him to impale himself on a glass tube. Powerful stuff!

A357. Max Von Sydow. Incidentally, a scene was supposedly filmed (but never appeared on-screen) in which Blofeld dies when his cat scratches him with a poison-laced claw. This would be the last appearance of Blofeld to date. The Broccoli Bond films have refused to use the character again due to legal complications with Kevin McClory, one of the producers of *Never Say Never Again*.

A358. The President of the United States

A359. The cash equivalent of 25 percent of their annual oil purchases

Answers

A360. Alec McCowan

A361. Algernon

A362. Nigel Small-Fawcett

A363. Four pounds—and an unknown number of "free radicals," which "M" had warned Bond cause toxic harm to the body.

A364. Bernie Casey, marking the only time to date the character has been played by a black actor

A365. Nicole, one of Bond's assistants in France. (How someone is placed *inside* a water bed is never actually explained, but it makes for an effective scene.)

A366. A double Bloody Mary with plenty of Worcestershire sauce

A367. $263,000. The shocking decision prompts Largo to ask Bond if he loses as graciously as he wins. 007 replies that he wouldn't know, as he never loses!

A368. Lani Hall, wife of Herb Alpert. Curiously, the two were involved with the musical scores for both "non-official" Bond films—*Casino Royale* and *Never Say Never Again*.

A369. She throws a snake onto his lap while he is driving, causing a fatal accident.

A370. Michel Legrand, providing one of the sparsest, least memorable scores imaginable

A371. "Some gratuitous sex and violence." To which 007 replies, "So do I!"

A372. Valerie Leon

A View to a Kill—Answers

A373. "California Girls"

A374. British rock group Gideon Park

A375. Sir Godfrey Tibbett, the film's sacrificial lamb

A376. "Project Main Strike"

A377. Chuck Lee (played by David Yip)

A378. Dolph Lundgren

A379. Jenny Flex

A380. Dr. Carl Mortner (Willoughby Gray), the Nazi scientist whose obscene experiments in genetics resulted in Zorin

A381. John Barry

A382. Duran Duran. The group supposedly approached Cubby Broccoli at a party and made the suggestion, and the result was the biggest Bond theme song in many years.

A383. Tanya Roberts

A384. Geologist (*Sure...*)

A385. Bond says he is a reporter for the *London Financial Times*.

A386. James Stock

A387. He is strangled in a car wash! (There's a lot of that going around!)

Answers

A388. He ingeniously lets air out from the tires and breathes from the inner tube.

A389. Atop the Golden Gate Bridge, where Zorin's blimp has become entangled

A390. W.G. Howe (Daniel Benzali, later to star in TV's *Murder One*). Zorin murders him anyway in a plan to cover up the proposed deaths he has in store for Bond and Stacey.

A391. It contains only rock salt. (It is never explained why one would keep a shotgun loaded with rock salt, or why Bond persists in firing at his enemies after he learns the gun is useless. By the way, why doesn't he just draw his weapon?)

A392. Pola Ivanova (played by Fiona Fullerton)

A393. Scarpine, Zorin's henchman

A394. The Order of Lenin

A395. $100 million per company plus half of their net income

A396. An omelet, but the yoke's on Bond as he doesn't get to score with her

A397. Achille Aubergine

A398. A blimp

A399. May Day, played by Grace Jones. Upon learning of her lover Zorin's plans to kill her, she heroically gives her life to save the day.

The Living Daylights—Answers

A400. Bratislava, Czechoslovakia

A401. Maryam d'Abo

A402. She is a renowned Czech cellist.

A403. General Koskov (Jeroen Krabbe), who promises MI 5 to spill his guts about the innermost secrets of the Soviet military. However, he is part of a plot to double-cross British Intelligence.

A404. Producer-screenwriter Michael G. Wilson. In fact, Wilson has appeared in every Bond film since *The Spy Who Loved Me,* although not necessarily in the flesh. He occasionally provides his voice only, depending on the circumstances. The Hitchcock-like play is based on the belief that Wilson's cameos are a good luck device, as well as an in-joke for the filmmakers.

A405. John Barry, longtime composer of 007 film scores, can be seen occasionally conducting the orchestra at the palatial opera house.

A406. Brad Whitaker (Joe Don Baker), a megalomaniac with an obsession with military history that inspires him to emulate the likes of Napoleon and Hitler

A407. Saunders, the by-the-book agent who disapproves of Bond and his methods. No sooner do the two finally learn to respect each other than Saunders is killed when an automatic door slams into him, the work of an enemy assassin. In the original script, Saunders was to have been cut in half, as evidenced by a line of dialogue Bond was to say. When someone says to call for an ambulance, 007 was to look at the body and note, "Make it two ambulances." The scene was cut, probably as it was decided to be needlessly grotesque.

A408. Thomas Wheatley

A409. Caroline Bliss, replacing the popular Lois Maxwell, who had appeared in every Bond film to date (at least those made by Eon Productions). Maxwell agreed that it would be inappropriate to have her flirting with much younger Timothy Dalton. She suggested, however, that the script be amended to introduce her as "M"! The producers refused, saying that it would be absurd to have a woman as head of British Intelligence. A decade later, they would enact that very strategy, having Pierce Brosnan's Bond report to a woman.

A410. At Harrod's Department Store. The package is filled with expensive goodies to soothe Koskov's nerves. However, Bond—ever the snob—can't resist replacing the wine with a superior brand—at MI 5's expense, of course.

A411. Kamran Shah, played with charismatic charm by Art Malik

A412. "A Ghetto Blaster." The boom box really does go "boom" and turns into a powerful miniature cannon.

A413. The recording group a-ha

A414. Barry Manilow. What's next—Bond and Moneypenny going on a date to the Liberace Museum?

A415. "If There Was a Man"

A416. The Pretenders sing it, and Chrissie Hynde wrote it to John Barry's music.

A417. Aston Martin Volante, and it is every bit as lethal as its notable predecessors. This vehicle contains such "extras" as rockets, skis, and a laser device which can separate an adversary's car frame from its chassis.

A418. John Rhys-Davies. The role was originally written for Walter Gotell in hopes of giving him his most prominent part to date as General Gogol. Unfortunately, Gotell became ill and could not get enough medical insurance, despite Cubby Broccoli's offer to pay for the cost. Much to Gotell's chagrin, the role was rewritten for Rhys-Davies. As a courtesy, Gotell was allowed to make a brief cameo at the end of the film. He subsequently recovered and resumed his acting career, and remains a close friend of Broccoli.

A419. The Rock of Gibraltar

A420. A milkman, although his wares are quite deadly. Using a number of bombs disguised as milk bottles, Necros launches an assault on MI 5 and successfully kidnaps Koskov, leaving the building in shambles.

A421. "The Lady Rose"

A422. "Hail, Britannia"

A423. Agent 004 dies when his lifeline is cut by an enemy agent as he scales a cliff.

A424. Tangiers

Licence to Kill—Answers

A425. In Mexico, with many interiors done at Churubusco Studios. The filmmakers had moved from Pinewood to save money. The shoot proved to be an ordeal, however, and the producers soon learned that whatever they saved in fees was lost due to problems working with the Mexican technicians and bureaucrats.

A426. Della Churchill (Priscilla Barnes). Bond serves as best man in their wedding and is driven to revenge when drug dealers kill her and mutilate Felix.

A427. A "Pip"-less Gladys Knight

A428. Michael Kamen

A429. Prof. Joe Butcher, a phony TV evangelist who acts as a cover for a drug cartel

A430. Pedro Armendariz Jr. His father played Kerim Bey in the second Bond movie and appeared in many John Ford films. While making *From Russia With Love,* he was suffering from terminal cancer. After filming wrapped, he immediately went into the hospital, where his pain was so great he shot himself.

A431. "If You Asked Me To," although most of Dion's fans probably don't realize the song originated in a Bond film

A432. It is the first movie title not taken from a Fleming novel. By this time, most of the marketable titles had been used. Only Fleming's short stories remained, and nearly all had titles with little value. The producers henceforth would create their own original titles, although they may still use elements and characters from Fleming's novels.

A433. Milton Krest, the drunken, slovenly, and corrupt skipper who meets a grisly end when Bond frames him as a betrayer of Sanchez

A434. Anthony Zerbe

A435. Pam Bouvier, the gun-toting, self-sufficient beauty who is more than a match for 007—both physically and intellectually

A436. "The Barrelhead." This was an actual bar located in Key West. It still retains an exhibit of photos from the shooting, as well as the hole through which Bond and Pam escape the bad guys!

A437. A cigarette lighter, which Bond refers to as a "genuine Felix lighter." Ironically, it is this everyday item—one not even "souped up" by "Q"—which saves Bond's life in his fight to the death with Sanchez.

A438. "He disagreed with something that ate him." In fact, Leiter's dismemberment by the shark actually appears in Fleming's novel *Live and Let Die*.

A439. Truman-Lodge, the effete yuppie who is slain by Sanchez in a fit of paranoia about traitors in his organization

A440. Kwang

A441. President Lopez, who inexplicably has become very chummy with MI 5. He's invited to their cocktail party, and gets to date Lupe even though when last seen he was a key operative for Sanchez!

A442. An iguana, the tail of which he uses to whip the unfaithful Lupe

A443. Sharkey (Frank McRae), the local MI 5 operative whose cover is that of a local fisherman

A444. Isthmus City, a rare fictional location for a Bond film

A445. Benecio Del Toro

A446. The ever-loyal "Q," who has taken leave to assist Bond when 007 is stripped of his license to kill. Despite his advancing years, this film provided Desmond Llewelyn with his longest—and best written—appearence to date.

A447. Robert Brown

A448. Killifer, who helps mastermind the escape and drives the prison van into the bay so Sanchez's men can rescue him

A449. Everett McGill

GoldenEye—Answers

A450. Agent 006. He and Bond are virtually brothers, thereby making his deception and betrayal all the more devastating to 007.

A451. General Ourumov (Gottfried John). He deceives his own military and steals the GoldenEye, in the process overseeing the slaughter of dozens of innocent people.

A452. Janus. Upon learning of Trevelyan's betrayal, the significance of Janus becomes clear to Bond: he was the two-faced god of ancient myth.

A453. It is the name of the house in Jamaica where Fleming would write the 007 novels.

A454. Jack Wade, a cynical, hard-bitten man who initially mocks the "stiff-assed Brit" with whom he is forced to work. Bond quickly earns his respect—by threatening him with a gun.

A455. Joe Don Baker

A456. Baker played the villainous arms dealer Brad Whitaker in *The Living Daylights*.

A457. BMW Roadster

A458. None. Strangely, although "Q" is allowed to describe the amazing gadgets, none are used in the film. In fact, given the huge hype for the BMW, it appears on-screen only fleetingly.

A459. Bond's friend Bill Tanner (played by Michael Kitchen)

A460. "M"—and with bosses like that, who needs enemies?

A461. Robbie Coltrane, the charismatic performer who appears all too briefly in *GoldenEye*. His short sequences leave the audience wanting to see more of him.

A462. Tina Turner sings it; Bono and The Edge of U2 wrote it.

A463. Eric Serra, who offers up one of the most bizarre Bond soundtracks ever, and was opposed to using the James Bond theme in the film! The one time the theme appears is in the tank chase, and this was scored at the last minute without Serra's participation.

A464. Dame Judi Deuch, a popular British musical comedy star

A465. She is known only as Caroline (Serena Gordon).

A466. "Straight up—with a twist," presumably like her men!

A467. Simonova is her last name; Izabella Scorupeo plays her.

A468. Dimitri Mishkin (Tcheky Karyo). Bond convinces him that Ouromov is a traitor, but the disclosure comes too late, as Mishkin is murdered by the once loyal general.

A469. Samantha Bond plays the Moneypenny of the 1990s—still rather dowdy, but definitely more independent. (The producers swear her name gave her no preference in testing for the role.)

A470. Jeffrey Caine and Bruce Feirstein—both first-time screenwriters. However, the story credit goes to Michael France, who wrote Stallone's *Cliffhanger*. As a teenager, France edited a home-grown Bond fan magazine called *Mr. Kiss-Kiss Bang-Bang*.

A471. In Cuba. In fact, the sequence was shot in Puerto Rico and the actual satellite set is an exact replica of one which exists on the island. (It is used to monitor for signs of alien life forms.)

A472. A Tiger helicopter, which can avoid radar detection

A473. St. Petersburg, Russia. The city was photographed from every angle, and Peter Lamont reconstructed an identical set back at Leavesden Studios in England. Indeed, the "fake" St. Petersburg is impossible to detect from shots of the real city which are interspersed within the tank chase.

A474. Miniature Effects supervisor Derek Meddings. His last great accomplishment was the miniatures used in the climax of *GoldenEye,* most notably the exact replica of the satellite dish. Meddings had worked on previous Bond films, and had received an Oscar nomination for *Moonraker.*

Top-Secret Multiple Choice Quiz—Answers

A475. C.

A476. B. "M" thwarts the brainwashed 007 by utilizing a bulletproof shield in his desk.

A477. C.

A478. C. Nelson played Bond as an American cardsharp, complete with crew cut!

A479. D. Fleming good-naturedly joked with the real Bond about "stealing" his name. The two men remained friends and corresponded for years.

A480. B. Jason Connery, Sean's son, played Fleming in *The Secret Life of Ian Fleming,* an original television movie made in 1990 by Ted Turner's Turner Pictures. The film had a theatrical release in Europe under the title *Spymaker.*

A481. C.

A482. B.

Answers

A483. C. The film infuriated Connery, who must have been relieved when his brother returned to an everyday life in Scotland. It had Neil's voice dubbed by someone who sounds like a Brooklyn thug. The movie has been a camp classic for years, and is available on video under the title *Double Double 0*. Incidentally, it features many Bond alumni, including Bernard Lee, Lois Maxwell, Daniela Bianchi, Adolfo Celi, and Anthony Dawson.

A484. B.

A485. D. A big-budget film version starring Dick Van Dyke was released in 1968, produced by Albert R. Broccoli—the only non-Bond film he has done since *Call Me Bwana*. The movie involved many of the technicians and writers from the Bond films, as well as Desmond Llewelyn in a small role.

A486. A.

A487. B. Fleming began to give advice to the show's producer Norman Felton, much to the dismay of Broccoli and Saltzman, who did not want the author involved with another spy property. In fact, the show's original title *Solo* was changed to *The Man From U.N.C.L.E.* when Broccoli and Saltzman pointed out that a character named Solo appears in *Goldfinger*. In the series, of course, the hero's name remained Napoleon Solo and he was played by Robert Vaughn.

A488. C. *Thunderball* was to be the first Bond film, but Fleming's involvement with a plagiarism suit over the novel made it too hot to touch at the time.

A489. B. The much-touted, but aborted project was cowritten by Connery and espionage writer Len Deighton and involved S.P.E.C.T.R.E. invading New York's sewer systems, as well as the Bermuda Triangle. The project was shelved when Cubby Broccoli filed lawsuits.

A490. B.

A491. A.

A492. D.

A493. D.

A494. B. Lazenby was the model seen in a Big Fry chocolate bar ad.

A495. B. Lazenby even drives an Aston Martin DB5 with "JB" license plates.

A496. C. Dalton admits he was too afraid to follow in Connery's footsteps, and he also feared—justifiably—that he was too young for the role at the time.

A497. C. Sean Connery (Oscar winner for *The Untouchables*), Christopher Walken (Oscar winner for *The Deer Hunter*), and composer John Barry, the multiple Oscar winner, who has a cameo in *The Living Daylights*.

A498. B. Bond does not wear a tux in *You Only Live Twice* and *Live and Let Die*.

A499. B. However, the actors were never in the same scene.

A500. C. Young felt the film was terrible and promised to make it up to Sean someday—which he obviously did. The two remained close friends until Young's death in 1994.

A501. B. Being committed to film several more episodes of *Remington Steele,* Brosnan lost the role—temporarily —to Timothy Dalton.

James Bond Fan Club and Memorabilia Information

The author would like to acknowledge that many of the facts contained in this book were based on information from the various James Bond fan club publications from around the world. The following are the major organizations which presently publish magazines devoted to the Bond phenomenon:

The James Bond Collectors Club, England
The James Bon Fan Club and Archive, England
Club James Bond 007, France
The Ian Fleming Foundation, a nonprofit group dedicated to preserving Fleming's works as well as reporting on the 007 films. The organization publishes the highly-praised *GoldenEye* magazine.

Each of these groups offers James Bond merchandise for sale through periodic catalogs. The single largest resource for Bond toys, books, posters, and other memorabilia is Spy Guise Inc. For one of their catalogs, along with information about how to join the above clubs, write to: SPY GUISE INC., Department T, POB 152, Dunellen, N.J. 08812.

More Citadel Entertainment Fun Facts and Interesting Trivia

Ask for any of these books at your bookstore. Or to order direct from the publisher, call 1-800-447-BOOK (MasterCard or Visa), or send a check or money order for the books purchased (plus $4.00 shipping and handling for the first book ordered and 75¢ for each additional book) to Carol Publishing Group, 120 Enterprise Avenue, Dept. 1793, Secaucus, NJ 07094.

The "Cheers" Trivia Book by Mark Wenger $9.95 paper (#51482)

Film Flubs: Memorable Movie Mistakes by Bill Givens $7.95 paper (#51161)

Also Available:
  Son of Film Flubs by Bill Givens $7.95 paper (#51279)

  Film Flubs: The Sequel by Bill Givens $7.95 paper (#51360)

Final Curtain: Deaths of Noted Movie and TV Personalities by Everett G. Jarvis $17.95 paper (#51646)

The "Seinfeld" Aptitude Test by Beth B. Golub $8.95 paper (#51583)

701 Toughest Movie Trivia Questions of All Time by William MacAdams and Paul Nelson $9.95 paper (#51700)

Starfleet Academy Entrance Exam by Peggy Robin $9.95 paper (#51695)

The TV Theme Song Trivia Book by Vincent Terrace $9.95 paper (#51786)

1,201 Toughest TV Trivia Questions of All Time by Vincent Terrace $9.95 paper (#51730)

The Ultimate Clint Eastwood Trivia Book by Lee Pfeiffer & Michael Lewis $8.95 paper (#51789)

The Ultimate James Bond Trivia Book by Michael Lewis $8.95 paper (#51793)

What's Your "Cheers" I.Q.? by Mark Wenger $9.95 paper (#51780)

What's Your "Frasier" I.Q.? by Robert Bly $8.95 paper (#51732)

What's Your "Friends" I.Q.? by Stephen Spignesi $9.95 paper (#51776)

What's Your "Mad About You" I.Q.? by Stephen Spignesi $8.95 paper #51682

Prices subject to change; books subject to availability